To the memory of Willis J. Potts, MD

CHICAGO

It Happened In Series

IT HAPPENED IN
CHICAGO

Scotti Cohn

Guilford, Connecticut

Copyright © 2009 by Morris Book Publishing, LLC

Project editor: David Legere
Text design: Nancy Freeborn
Map: M.A. Dubé © Morris Book Publishing, LLC
Photo of World's Fair, Chicago, 1893 courtesy Library of Congress

Library of Congress Cataloging-in-Publication Data
Cohn, Scotti.
 It happened in Chicago / Scotti Cohn.
     p. cm. — (It happened in series)
 Includes bibliographical references.
 ISBN 978-0-7627-5056-6
 1. Chicago (Ill.)—History—Anecdotes. I. Title.
 F548.36.C645 2009
 977.3'11—dc22
                              2009018283

Printed in the United States of America

10 9 8 7 6 5 4 3 2 1

CONTENTS

CONTENTS

ACKNOWLEDGMENTS

I am grateful to the following individuals and organizations who helped me create *It Happened in Chicago:* Charlie Maze, for suggesting the chapter about Red Grange; Donald Perrot, Intertribal Spiritual Leader, for taking time to correspond with me about the history of the Potawatomi in Chicago; *Chicago Tribune; Chicago Sun-Times;* Chicago Historical Society; Jane Addams Hull House Association; The Provident Foundation; Illinois State Historical Society; Eastland Disaster Historical Society.

Special thanks go to my editor, Erin Turner, for her unwavering encouragement and unerring ability to determine what should stay and what should go.

Finally, I must thank Dr. Willis Potts of Chicago's Children's Memorial Hospital. In the course of his long career in medicine, Dr. Potts treated many different disorders and conditions. In 1951 he was asked to examine a 15-month-old child who had a tumor the size of a softball near the base of her spine. Her parents had been told that she might not live. If she lived, they were warned, there was a strong chance that she would never walk. After examining the tiny patient, Dr. Potts calmly answered their questions:

"Will she live?" they asked.

"Of course she'll live," he answered firmly.

"Will she be able to walk?"

"Of course she'll be able to walk."

He was right on both counts.

Fifty-eight years later, I am still going strong, thanks in no small part to Dr. Willis Potts and Children's Memorial Hospital.

INTRODUCTION

As a child growing up in Springfield, Illinois, in the 1950s, I have fond memories of my visits to Chicago. I vividly recall my first ride on the "L," Brookfield Zoo, the amazing Christmas decorations in the downtown store windows, and the house on South Ada Street where my aunt, uncle, and three cousins lived.

When I told friends and family I was writing a book called *It Happened in Chicago,* their responses included:

"Is there anything that *didn't* happen in Chicago?"

"What happens in Chicago, stays in Chicago."

"Chicago! Chicago! That toddlin' town!" (usually sung loudly and off-key)

Like those responses, the events covered in this book range from the sad to the strange to the sublime, with brief stops at silly, sobering, and spectacular. *It Happened in Chicago* is not, however, a comprehensive history of the city. If you are looking for that type of book, I recommend *City of the Century* by Donald Miller or *City of Big Shoulders: A History of Chicago* by Robert G. Spinney. My General Sources list in the Bibliography provides other options you may want to consider. If you are looking for an entertaining account of some of the Windy City's most interesting events, this is the book for you.

In my research, I came across far more events than I could possibly cover in this book. I hope you will enjoy reading about the ones that I included rather than lamenting those I omitted.

Perhaps you'll discover, as I did, that there really isn't much that *didn't* happen in Chicago!

PUTTING DOWN ROOTS

1779

In the early seventeenth century, there was no "stormy, husky, brawling City of the Big Shoulders" on the shore of the vast, clear lake that stretched as far as the eye could see. There were forests and rivers and sand dunes, and the voices of native tribes echoed among the oaks and pines. The smoke from their fires rose into the skies over marshes and prairies. Their feet made impressions in the soft, dark earth beside lakes and streams. They grew maize and foraged for wild berries. Armed with spears and bows and arrows, they hunted beasts, birds, and fish.

At the western tip of the great lake was a place the native people called *Eshegago*—place of the wild onion. They constructed no large villages on that swampy, sandy ground, but their most important trails intersected there. It was a trade area and a refuge, a perfect spot to replenish themselves on their travels.

In 1673, when Father Jacques Marquette and Louis Jolliet journeyed down from Canada into the Illinois country, the natives showed them one of their trade routes connecting Lake Michigan with the Mississippi River. The word spread quickly about the Chicago Portage or the "Portage de Chicagau," as René-Robert Cavelier, Sieur de La Salle, referred to it ten years later.

"This will be the gate of empire," he predicted, "this the seat of commerce."

First, however, someone had to do more than simply visit Eshegago. Someone needed to put down roots there. Woodsmen, trappers, and missionaries continued to pass through the area, but seldom stayed very long. Sometime between 1772 and 1779, Jean Baptiste Point de Sable (also written as Point du Sable or Du Sable) arrived. Regarded as Chicago's first permanent settler, he lived at the head of the Chicago River for almost twenty years.

No one knows for certain where he came from. Some say Santo Domingo or Haiti; others think Quebec is more likely. Some believe he was educated in France. One account makes him a runaway slave from Kentucky. His ancestry is commonly believed to be Haitian and French. We do know that in 1778, Jean Baptiste Point de Sable married a Potawatomi woman named Catherine in a Catholic ceremony in Cahokia, Illinois, about two hundred and eighty miles from Chicago.

In 1779, during the American Revolution, Colonel Arent Schuyler DePeyster, British commander at Fort Mackinac, reported an encounter with "Baptiste Point DeSable, a handsome Negro, well educated and settled at Eschikagou."

A few months after that, British lieutenant Thomas Bennett reported to his commander: "I had the negro, Baptiste Point au Sable, brought prisoner from the river Du Chemin" (near present-day Michigan City, Indiana). Point de Sable was apparently arrested as an American sympathizer, but Bennett noted that he "in every respect behaved in a manner becoming to a man in his situation, and has many friends who give him a good character."

In the spring of 1790, British trader Hugh Heward was entertained by Point de Sable at Chicago. Heward wrote in his diary that Point de Sable provided his party with flour, pork, and bread. As historian Thomas A. Meehan has noted, this suggests that Point de Sable was fairly well established by that time, since he "evidently had hogs, fields under cultivation, his own flour mill, and also someone to bake bread."

Accounts from other travelers indicate that the dark-skinned entrepreneur was still in the area four years later. Fur trader Augustin Grignon wrote:

> *My brother, Perish Grignon, visited Chicago about 1794 and told me that Pointe de Saible* [sic] *was a large man, that he had a commission for some office, but for what particular office or for what government I cannot now recollect. He was a trader, pretty wealthy, and drank freely.*

We get a better idea of how impressive Point de Sable's operation was from the document listing the property he sold to Jean Lalime in 1800. It describes "an establishment consisting of a house 40 by 22 feet in size, a horsemill 36 by 24 feet, a bakehouse 20 by 18 feet, a dairy 10 feet square, a smokehouse 8 feet square, a poultry house 15 feet square, a workshop 15 by 12 feet, one stable 30 by 24 feet, a barn 40 by 28 feet, and all the wood necessary for a new barn."

Point de Sable also sold Lalime a wide range of farming implements and livestock, including two mules, thirty head of cattle, two spring calves, thirty-eight hogs, and forty-four hens. The list of household furnishings reveals that Point de Sable was a man of taste and refinement. As Meehan observed: "Only such a man would have thought of having a feather bed, a cabinet of French walnut, a couch, and a bureau, to say nothing of mirrors and pictures, in the midst of a wilderness."

After he departed from Chicago in 1800, Point de Sable settled in St. Charles, Missouri. By 1813, he was ill and impoverished, having lost nearly everything in various real estate transactions. His burial in the parish cemetery of St. Charles Borromeo was recorded on August 29, 1818. No mention was made of his wife or his two children, Jean Baptiste Point de Sable Jr. and Suzanne. Many historians believe they were no longer living.

Point de Sable's importance to Chicago is seen in the names of numerous places and institutions, including Du Sable High School, the Du Sable Museum of African American History, and Du Sable Harbor. A city ordinance passed in 2006 officially recognized Point de Sable's contribution as part of the celebration of Chicago's 169th birthday. Point de Sable's farm and trading post were located where the Tribune Tower now stands.

ORDERED TO EVACUATE

1812

The message came to Captain Nathan Heald, commanding officer at Fort Dearborn, one afternoon in August in 1812. Although the weather was oppressively hot, Heald felt a chill run through him as he read the orders, signed by William Hull, brigadier general of the Army of the Northwest:

> *Sir:—It is with regret I order the Evacuation of your Post owing to the want of Provisions. . . You will therefore Destroy all arms & ammunition, but the Goods of the Factory you may give to the Friendly Indians who may be desirous of Escorting you on to Fort Wayne & to the Poor & needy of your Post.*

Heald frowned. The local Potawatomi tribe had been friendly in the past. However, in recent years hostility toward settlers had intensified. Many of the Potawatomi now supported Tecumseh, a leader of the Shawnee who declared that all red men must "unite in claiming a common and equal right in the land as it was at first, and should be now—for it never was divided, but belongs to all."

In November 1811, American troops led by William Henry Harrison had fought the followers of Tecumseh and his brother, Tenskwatawa, also known as The Prophet, near the Tippecanoe River in the Indiana Territory. The two sides suffered nearly equal losses, but the battle was widely regarded as an American victory.

Fort Dearborn stood on land acquired by the U.S. government from American Indians in the 1795 Treaty of Greenville, described as "a piece of land six miles square at the mouth of the Chicago river, emptying into the southwest end of Lake Michigan." Since the fort's erection in 1803, settlers and Indians nearby had lived in relative harmony.

Following the Battle of Tippecanoe, relations between settlers and the Indians near Fort Dearborn began to deteriorate. In April 1812, warriors from the Winnebago tribe killed two men at a farmhouse near the fort. Two other white men escaped and warned people at neighboring homes, including the family of John Kinzie, a man long held in high regard by the natives. The Kinzies and other civilians fled to Fort Dearborn. Inhabitants of the fort were advised to be on the alert for bands of Winnebago and young Potawatomi who resented the way their elders accommodated whites. These renegades roamed the frontier, stealing livestock and burning buildings.

The tension between settlers and Indians was further amplified in June 1812, when the United States declared war on Great Britain in response to British violations of U.S. maritime rights. The British actively recruited Indians, offering large numbers of Indians gifts of guns and money for their allegiance. In July, British troops aided by Indian allies seized highly strategic Fort Mackinac in Michigan.

All of this was on Captain Heald's mind on August 9, as he read Hull's orders to evacuate Fort Dearborn.

In addition to fifty-five soldiers and a dozen male civilians, the fort housed nine women (including Heald's wife, Rebecca Wells Heald) and eighteen children. Heald's officers questioned the wisdom of an evacuation, but Heald was unwilling to go against Hull's orders. As preparations went forward, the number of Indians surrounding Fort Dearborn swelled to an estimated five hundred to seven hundred. Heald held council with their leaders. The chiefs agreed that the Indians would escort the settlers safely to Fort Wayne. In payment, they would receive a sizeable reward, along with everything the settlers left behind at the fort.

What Heald failed to understand was that the leaders he met with no longer had absolute control over their men.

On August 13, Captain William Wells (Rebecca Heald's uncle) arrived from Fort Wayne to help with the evacuation. He brought with him thirty pro-American Miami braves. Wells was white but had been brought up by Indians and had married a Miami chief's daughter.

Soldiers broke apart the extra weapons and ammunition stored at Fort Dearborn and threw them into an abandoned well. They dumped the fort's liquor supply into the river. Finally, they distributed the remaining provisions, goods, and livestock among the Indians.

On the morning of August 15, Captain Wells rode out through the stockade gate, his face blacked in the manner of an Indian going to battle. Behind him rode about fifteen Miami warriors wearing war paint. Soldiers and militia came next, followed by a short train of wagons carrying supplies, women, children, and the sick and disabled. In all, the white settlers numbered just under one hundred. Bringing up the rear were the remainder of the Miamis.

Approximately five hundred Potawatomi and Winnebago braves formed a line to the right of the column led by Wells. The procession headed due south along an old Indian trail, parallel with the Chicago River. When the group came to a row of sand hills that separated the beaches of Lake Michigan from the prairie, the soldiers and their charges continued along the beach. The braves, led by Chief Black-bird, filed to the right, disappearing behind the ridges of sand.

A mile and a half from Fort Dearborn, sudden activity at the head of the line sent waves of alarm through the caravan of anxious travelers. Margaret Helm, the seventeen-year-old wife of Lieutenant Lina T. Helm, later described what happened next:

> *Captain Wells, who had kept somewhat in advance*
> *of his Miamis, came riding furiously back. "They are*
> *about to attack us!" he shouted. "Form instantly and*
> *charge upon them." Scarcely were the words uttered*
> *when a volley was showered from among the sand-hills.*
> *The troops were hastily brought into line and charged*
> *up the bank.*

The Miamis departed. Potawatomi and Winnebago fired down on the wagon train over the edge of the ridge. Several slashed their way with tomahawks through the crowd of soldiers and settlers. Lieutenant Helm wrote an account of the attack in which he described horrors witnessed by John Kinzie:

> *The Indians came down on the baggage waggons for*
> *Plunder, they Butchered every male citizen but Kenzie,*
> *[and killed] two women & 12 Children in the most*
> *inhuman manner Possible.*

It took only about fifteen minutes for the Indians to overcome the settlers. Captain Heald, wounded twice, retreated with his remaining men to a small elevation in the open prairie, out of range of the sand bank. The decision was made to surrender on the condition that the lives of the prisoners would be spared. Heald offered the Indians a ransom of one hundred dollars for every prisoner still living.

"We were taken back to their encampment near the fort," Heald wrote later, "and distributed among the different tribes. The next morning, they set fire to the fort and left the place, taking the prisoners with them."

Captain Wells died in the massacre. Heald estimated that the enemy lost fifteen men. He reported his own losses as "twenty-six regulars and all the militia . . . with two women and twelve children." Critics of Heald's actions suggested that destroying the arms, ammunition, and liquor had incited the Indians to violence.

"If we had not destroyed those items," Heald replied, "every single white person would have been killed."

Of the twenty-seven regulars who survived, eighteen were eventually returned to civilization. The same was true for six of the seven women who survived. Five of the six surviving children were returned to civilization with their mothers. The entire Kinzie family was spared. Mrs. Helm credited Black Partridge, a friendly Potawatomi, with rescuing her from certain death.

On December 24, 1814, Great Britain and America signed the Treaty of Ghent, in which they agreed to return to the status quo from before the war.

Fort Dearborn was rebuilt in 1816. It was abandoned again in 1836, but remained standing until 1856. A bronze marker in the pavement at Michigan Avenue and Wacker Drive marks the approximate site of both the first and second Fort Dearborns.

FAREWELL TO *ESHEGAGO*

1835

From a second-story window in Chicago's Sauganash Hotel, John Caton watched warriors from the Potawatomi nation gather at the Council House. They had painted their foreheads, cheeks, and noses with stripes of vermilion, and entwined feathers from the eagle and the hawk into their coarse black hair. Some of them beat on hollow vessels or struck sticks together. Others yelled, waving tomahawks and war clubs, distorting their faces into expressions of anger and hatred. Eight hundred strong, they leaped and danced under the blazing sun of an August afternoon in 1835.

Caton was no stranger to Chicago or to the Potawatomi, who called themselves Bodewadmi, "Keeper of the Fire." He knew many of the warriors and their families personally. Recalling the scene in August 1835, he wrote:

> *They appreciated that [the war dance] was their last*
> *on their native soil—that it was a sort of funeral cer-*
> *emony of old associations and memories, and nothing*

was omitted to lend it all the grandeur and solemnity possible.

In 1835, the Potawatomi were the principal Native American residents of the Chicago area, having taken over the region from other tribes around the end of the seventeenth century. They called Chicago *Eshegago,* meaning "place of the wild onions." Historians point out that Native Americans did not establish large settlements or villages on the exact spot where present-day Chicago is located. As historian Virgil J. Vogel put it: "While native people came here to use local resources, they had better sense than to subject themselves to local wind, cold and marshes."

During the early decades of the eighteenth century, Native Americans in the Chicago area had fought among themselves and against white settlers and trappers. The Treaty of Greenville, signed in 1795, was the first of what would be many forced cessations of land by Native Americans to the United States. It included a "piece of land six miles square at the mouth of the Chikago river, emptying into the southwest end of Lake Michigan" where Fort Dearborn was erected in 1803. In the ensuing decades, settlers continued to pour into the area. With them came military forces with orders to keep native populations under control. Several treaties divested Native Americans of additional lands in the region. The Blackhawk War in 1832 all but sealed their fate.

By September 1833, the chiefs and headmen of the Potawatomi had realized it was time to cut their losses. If they had to evacuate the region—which seemed likely—they wanted to negotiate the timing, conditions, and compensation. They gathered in Eshegago for a preliminary council with U.S. government representatives. Word of the 1833 treaty negotiations drew traveler Charles Joseph Latrobe to Chicago. Latrobe wrote of the scene that greeted him there: "The grassy prairie teemed with figures; warriors mounted or on foot, squaws, and horses.

Here a race between three or four Indian ponies, each carrying a double rider, whooping and yelling . . . Indian dogs and children. . ."

Also on hand for the festivities were thousands of what Latrobe called "horse-dealers, and horse-stealers, rogues of every description . . . men pursuing Indian claims . . . sharpers of every degree." They were there to profit as best they could from the situation. "With all this," Latrobe concluded, "the whites seemed to me to be more pagan than the red men."

Arriving on September 14, the Potawatomi chiefs and headmen had spent a week discussing the proposal among themselves. Latrobe described "companies of old warriors under every bush, smoking, arguing, palavering, powwowing, with great earnestness."

Latrobe also noted that plenty of whiskey was available for sale on the grounds, and that drunkenness was the order of the day for many of the Indians. This he considered a grievous thing that the government commissioners should have prevented. "As long as it can be said with truth," he wrote, "that drunkenness was not guarded against, and that the means were furnished at the very time of the treaty, and under the very nose of the Commissioners, how can it be expected but a stigma will attend every transaction of this kind."

Council meetings were held in a spacious open shed in a meadow across the river from Fort Dearborn. Latrobe observed "twenty or thirty chiefs present, seated at the lower end of the enclosure; while the Commissioners, Interpreters, &c. were at the upper."

On September 26, 1833, three U.S. government representatives and more than seventy-five Native American leaders signed the Treaty of Chicago. It stipulated that the "United Nation of Chippewa, Ottowa and Potawatamie Indians" would cede five million acres of land to the United States. Tradition held that the Chippewa (Ojibwe), Ottawa (Odawa), and Potawatomi were originally part of the same nation, which they called *Neshnabek,* meaning "True or Original People."

The Native Americans also agreed to abandon the Great Lakes area entirely "as soon as conveniently can be done." The treaty specified that the United States would move them to their new territory at its own expense, providing subsistence while upon the journey and for one year after their arrival.

In return for their concessions, the Native Americans would receive "a tract of country west of the Mississippi river . . . to be not less in quantity than five millions of acres." They also received money, goods, and provisions.

Although compensation was made in part in 1833, a portion was withheld pending official ratification of the treaty by the President and Senate of the United States. The process took nearly two years. In August 1835 the Potawatomi returned to Eshegago to receive the next installment of their payment and to bid farewell to their homeland.

Within three years, most of the Potawatomi had left Eshegago for Wisconsin, Missouri, Iowa, and Canada. Billy Caldwell (called "Sauganash," said to mean "Englishman") was rewarded with a lifetime annuity for his help in treaty negotiations. He moved west with other members of the tribe, where he continued to play a leadership role until his death from cholera six years later.

Writing in 1990, Terry Straus noted:

> *Although historians commonly represent the fact that the Potawatomi were pushed out of Illinois, the Potawatomi are still here in Illinois, and have been here for well over two hundred years. Intertribal marriage was one of the ways the Potawatomi remained in this area, and then later on through the government's Relocation Act.*

Today there are several active bands of Potawatomi living in various states as well as Canada.

UP, UP, AND HOORAY!

1856

Built on the shore of Lake Michigan, Chicago in the mid-nineteenth century was a filthy place. With city streets barely above the water table, thoroughfares were buried in mud throughout the town. The situation was so bad that people joked about it. As one story went, a man was passing by when he saw another man shoulder-deep in mud. The first man asked "Can I help you?" The second man replied, "No, thank you. I have a good horse under me."

But the filth wasn't really a joking matter. In 1854 in Chicago the death toll from cholera reached 1,424—more than 2 percent of the city's population. It was enough to spur Chicagoans to organize a public meeting to address the problem. At the time, it was not known that cholera is caused by bacteria and the toxins they produce. The disease was thought to be caused by dirty water and so-called "death fogs"—fumes produced by exposed sewage.

Hoping to improve conditions, the city covered streets and sidewalks with cross-pieces of heavy timber atop which they placed wooden planks. It wasn't a bad idea in theory. Unfortunately, nails in the rough boards caught the hems of fashionable hoop skirts, causing women to fall and injure themselves. Underneath the planks, garbage and animal waste mixed with standing water. The odor was appalling, especially in summer. As timbers rotted and warped, they trapped the loathsome brew, which soon became rat infested. When a carriage rumbled over the deteriorating boards, foul water spurted into the air.

In 1855, the newly formed Board of Sewerage Commissioners brought Boston engineer Ellis S. Chesbrough to Chicago. He advised the Commissioners that the level of Chicago's streets was too low to adequately drain the new sewers. He recommended what must have seemed like a radical, perhaps even crazy solution: raising the grade of the streets six to ten feet.

By the spring of 1856 Chesbrough had convinced the Commissioners that establishing a new grade was the only way to lift Chicago out of the muck once and for all. First the Chicago River was dredged to deepen it for sewage. Next the dredged soil was used to raise the street level high enough to cover sewer pipes. New guttered streets were paved with stone or cedar block.

Raising the streets meant that everything else—horsecar tracks, lampposts, trees, hydrants—had to be elevated as high as twelve feet. Owners of buildings were responsible for lifting their structures to meet the new street level. Large crowds routinely gathered to stare in fascination as shops, factories, and sometimes entire city blocks were hoisted aloft. On January 26, 1858, the *Chicago Daily Tribune* described the raising of a brick structure on the corner of Randolph and Dearborn Streets:

> *The building is of brick, four stories high, forty by seventy feet, and its estimated weight is about seven hundred and fifty tons. The building was raised*

*up bodily six feet and two inches, some two hun-
dred screws and fifteen men being employed in the
operation.*

The raising of Chicago took about twenty years to complete. In May 1860, the *Tribune* announced that the Tremont Hotel, a "solid mass of six story brick buildings, covering over an acre" would be raised to grade. Work commenced in January 1861. Among the firms hired to accomplish the feat was a company owned by George M. Pullman, who would later become famous as the inventor of the Pullman sleeping car for use on railroads.

Pullman, a cabinet-maker and construction contractor from New York, was frequently in demand. As described by Donald Miller, Pullman's procedure was so carefully coordinated it could be considered "elegant."

*He would have workmen dig holes into the foundation
of a building then place heavy timbers under it. Each
of the several hundred men was put in charge of four or
more jackscrews. When all was ready, George Pullman,
standing in the street, would blow a whistle, the signal
for brother Albert to order the men to give each of their
jacks a turn. As the building rose slowly, almost imper-
ceptibly, it was shored up with wood pilings; and great
numbers of masons, working at terrific speed, would lay
new footings under it.*

The *Tribune* reported that work on the Tremont House would begin about the first to the tenth of February. On February 12, 1861, the paper assured readers that "improvement is progressing as fast as money and men can make it."

As if the lifting of such a monstrosity was not impressive enough, the task was completed without interrupting the daily business of the hotel. One guest declared that he was only aware of what was happening because the stairway from the street into the hotel grew steeper each day, and the lower windows, which had been level with his face when he checked in, were three or four feet higher when he checked out. The Tremont House formally reopened in July but, as newspapers made sure to note, activities in the hotel went on "as usual" during the entire renovation and elevation process.

By then, Civil War news had replaced stories about the raising of Chicago on the front page of local newspapers. The week the Tremont House reopened, Union and Confederate troops fought the first great battle of the War—the Battle of First Bull Run or the First Battle of Manassas—which ended in a Southern victory.

The technology required to raise the city of Chicago was also used to lift and transport buildings across town. When Scotsman David McCrae visited Chicago in 1867, the sights, sounds, and smells of the city astonished him. He marveled at the grain elevators, housed in "a stupendous building, 110 feet high, presenting the appearance of a mountain boxed up for transit." He was awed by the stockyards, with their "application of steam-power in the conversion of pigs into pork." He was shocked by the city's "worldliness and wickedness," and noted that "her good people are very good, her bad people are very bad."

In his book, *The Americans at Home*, he wrote:

> *The first thing that attracted my attention when driving from the station to one of the hotels was the sight*

of a two-story house moving up the street before us. I
pointed it out in amazement to the driver.

"Did you never see a house moving before?" said he
unconcernedly.

"No. Do your houses move about like that?"

"Wall," he said, "there's always some of them on
the move."

In 1873, Chicago suffered another cholera epidemic. This time, only 116 deaths were reported, and those tended to be in densely populated areas where sanitation laws were not observed. Continued improvements in public health eventually eradicated the disease.

A PARTY IN THE GREAT WIGWAM

1860

The two-story "wigwam" under construction at the corner of Lake and Market Streets in April 1860 was the perfect place for a party—the Republican Party, to be exact. Built on the site of Chicago's first hotel, the Sauganash, the rectangular wood structure was designed to hold about ten thousand people. It had an immense floor area, abundant windows, and deep galleries running around three sides.

Back in March, the *Chicago Press and Tribune* had reported:

> *The proposition to build a comodious* [sic] *temporary structure for the accommodation of the Republican National Convention and, for the convenience of the Republicans of Cook County during the campaign, meets with universal favor.*

In naming the structure, the newspaper followed the custom of the day, which was to call a political campaign headquarters a "wigwam." Throughout March and April and into May, the *Press and Tribune* regularly reported construction progress, and readers soon got used to seeing articles titled "THE GREAT WIGWAM."

Two days before the grand opening, the ladies of Chicago decorated the hall with red, white, and blue draperies and evergreen wreaths. Huge paintings of Liberty, Plenty, Justice, and so forth appeared on arched panels at the rear of the space. The pillars that supported the roof were entwined with red, white, and blue streamers.

"When, for the first time the effect of gas light was added," gushed the *Press and Tribune,* "the effect was brilliant in the extreme."

One reason Chicago worked well as a site for the 1860 convention was the number of hotels: forty-two, according to historian P. Orman Ray. Further, a dozen railroad lines reached Chicago, offering convenient transportation for delegates. Chicago—population 109,263—was becoming a "real city." Some of the streets were even paved. However, those who pushed hardest to hold the Republican Convention in Chicago had another reason—one that would become apparent as time passed.

Of all the candidates under consideration for the Republican nomination, one stood out as the most likely winner: Senator William Henry Seward, former governor of New York. Informal ballots taken by delegates on trains rumbling toward Chicago showed Seward ahead of all other candidates by margins such as 210 to 30, 127 to 44, and 113 to 41.

One by one the trains pulled into the Chicago station. Marching clubs of young men, known as the Wide-Awakes, escorted delegations to their various headquarters. Rockets, cannons, trumpets, and rousing cheers welcomed newcomers. Hotels filled up, then overflowed. People slept on billiard tables and were glad to have them.

According to some estimates, Chicago's population may have doubled during convention week. As one might expect, the less savory elements of society took full advantage. The *Press and Tribune* cautioned: "[T]he light fingered fraternity have sent delegates. Look out for them. A passenger on the Galena and Chicago Union Railroad had his pockets picked of $160."

On Wednesday, May 16, 1860, at 12:10 p.m., the second Republican National Convention in history was called to order in the Wigwam. About forty-five hundred people stood shoulder to shoulder in front of the stage. The galleries—with room for three thousand—were packed. Historian Ray later observed that even the *Chicago Times,* a Democratic newspaper, had to admit that the representatives were "perhaps as fine a looking body of men as ever assembled in the Union."

Seward had his share of detractors. Many feared that his ardent anti-slavery position would alienate too many voters. Other reasons for opposition to Seward included his strong stance against nativism (the anti-immigrant movement) and his connection to New York State political boss Thurlow Weed.

On Thursday morning, May 17, the Seward delegates marched from their hotel to the Wigwam accompanied by a uniformed band playing the song "Oh, Isn't He a Darling." That afternoon, the assembly adopted a party platform. The throng in the Wigwam responded with such enthusiasm that, according to Ohio journalist Murat Halstead, "a herd of buffaloes or lions could not have made a more tremendous roaring." A motion was made to proceed to ballot for a candidate for the presidency. However, the printer had not yet delivered the papers needed for keeping the tally. The convention was adjourned until Friday. At Seward's headquarters, delegates toasted the candidate's impending victory with champagne.

Among those who did not celebrate with the Seward delegates were Norman Judd, chairman of the Illinois delegation; Joseph Medill, editor of the *Chicago Daily Press and Tribune;* and Judge David Davis of Bloomington, Illinois. They had no intention of allowing Seward to be selected. Judd had lobbied tirelessly for the convention to be held in Chicago because he knew that would give the home-field advantage to Illinois' "favorite son": Abraham Lincoln.

Given Seward's popularity, Lincoln's backers had their work cut out for them. A caucus of the delegations from New Jersey, Pennsylvania, Indiana, and Illinois met on Thursday afternoon to determine if they could all get behind a single candidate to defeat Seward. Lincoln was by no means unknown to them. He had won considerable support in New England following a speech to the Young Men's Central Republican Union of New York in February and had subsequently made speeches in New Hampshire, Rhode Island, and Connecticut.

The caucus could not reach a consensus. Reluctant to give up, they appointed a committee consisting of three delegates from each of the four states. The twelve men dialogued into the wee hours of Friday morning. Eventually they agreed that Lincoln was a stronger candidate than any of the other "favorite sons" entered in the competition. They also decided that Lincoln stood a better chance than Seward of being elected president over any Democratic candidate.

Friday morning, Seward supporters staged another grand march through town with their brass band. With scarlet feathers waving and trumpets blaring, they arrived at the Wigwam, only to find it almost full. The night before, Lincoln's men had given out hundreds of counterfeit admission tickets to Lincoln supporters who, arriving early as instructed, had filled the hall. Not only that, Judd and Medill made sure that the New York delegates who did get in were seated far off to one side, away from key swing states such as Pennsylvania. As an added touch, Lincoln's backers planted two men with exceptionally loud voices to lead the cheering whenever his name was mentioned.

When William M. Evarts of New York nominated Seward, the crowd applauded enthusiastically. Judd rose from his seat.

"I desire, on behalf of the delegation from Illinois, to put in nomination as a candidate for president of the United States, Abraham Lincoln of Illinois."

The response, according to Halstead, "was prodigious, rising and raging far beyond the Seward shriek."

Then Austin Blair of Michigan seconded the nomination of Seward.

"The shouting was absolutely frantic, shrill and wild," Halstead wrote. "Hundreds of persons stopped their ears in pain."

Caleb B. Smith of Indiana seconded the nomination of Lincoln.

"The uproar that followed was beyond description," Halstead declared. "The Lincoln boys . . . gave a concentrated shriek that was positively awful, and accompanied it with stamping that made every plank and pillar in the building quiver."

Three ballots later, Seward's followers sat in stunned silence. Lincoln was just one and a half votes away from the number needed to win the nomination. Suddenly D. K. Cartter of Ohio sprang up and announced the change of four Ohio votes to Lincoln. A secretary, tally sheet in hand, exclaimed, "Fire the salute! Abe Lincoln is nominated!"

With Hannibal Hamlin as his running mate, Lincoln was elected the sixteenth president of the United States on November 6, 1860, defeating Stephen Douglas, John Bell, and John C. Breckinridge.

City groups used the wigwam for other large meetings before it burned down, probably in the Great Chicago Fire of 1871. By the time the twenty-first century rolled around, Chicago had hosted more than two dozen Republican and Democratic National Conventions. Modern tourists can find the location of The Great Wigwam at the corner of Lake Street and Wacker Drive.

"THE CITY OF THE WEST IS DEAD!"

1871

On the night of October 8, 1871, shouts of alarm roused Catherine O'Leary from a deep sleep. Her husband, Patrick, muttered and rolled over. The next shout caused both of the O'Learys to sit straight up in bed.

"Fire! Fire!"

As they dashed out the door of their one-story frame cottage, a gust of wind blasted thick, acrid smoke into their faces. Catherine and Patrick stumbled through dense, oven-hot air into an alley that served as a street in their neighborhood on Chicago's poverty-stricken West Side. Catherine collided with neighbor Denis Ryan.

"Fire!" he croaked. "Your barn . . . the loft . . . couldn't get animals out!"

Catherine turned toward the stable where she and Patrick kept five cows and a horse. She and her daughter had milked the cows at 4:30 that afternoon, fed the horse, and put all of animals in the barn at about 7:00 that night.

"Grab your buckets!" Patrick shouted to the neighbors who had begun to gather around. "We've got to throw water on the house or it'll go up as well!"

They knew the drill. Fires were routine in a world where wood was the most common building material. Roofs were constructed of highly flammable pine chips and tar. Sidewalks were made of pine or hemlock planking. Streets were raised on wooden supports. Reporter Joseph Edgar Chamberlain described the O'Learys' community as "thickly studded with one-story frame dwellings, cow stables, pig sties, corncribs, sheds innumerable; every wretched building within four feet of its neighbor, and everything of wood." The unusually dry summer and fall of 1871 had raised the odds that something somewhere would catch fire.

A storekeeper near the O'Leary house tried to turn in an alarm, but the fire-alarm box failed to work. The crew of the nearest engine company dashed to the scene, but additional assistance was delayed because a watchman telegraphed the wrong location to the rest of the fire department.

From the O'Learys' barn on the near West Side, the fire moved north and east, toward the Chicago River. Flames jumped the river at about midnight, and the inferno headed northeast. Its progress was aided by convection whirls, created when superheated columns of extremely hot air combined with cooler descending air. These tornado-like "fire devils" could tear the roof off a building and fling it a quarter of a mile.

After evening church services on Sunday, October 8, Mrs. Alfred Hebard, visiting from Iowa, went to the upper story of the Palmer House hotel with her husband and daughter. They saw the fire but retired to their rooms after deciding that it would not cross the river. Mrs. Hebard tried to go to sleep, but was soon startled by someone rapping on every door along the hallway. She and her family learned that the Palmer House was in great danger. They fled to a cousin's house "amid a shower of coals driven by the furious wind from burning buildings and lumber yards, and which, seeming to be caught by an eddy, were whirled in our faces."

Shortly after 2:00 Monday morning, high school principal George Howland was awakened by his brother. Howland looked outside, but saw no reason to be overly alarmed. He invited his brother in for a cup of coffee.

"I was just pouring my coffee," Howland wrote later, "when hearing a crackling, I went to the door and found the roof all on fire."

Like Howland, people all over the city were getting wake-up calls. The Great Fire grew as a furious wind drove the heat onward in sheets of flame. Crowds of people forged through dense smoke and blinding dust, dragging trunks, bundles, and children.

Mary Fales, wife of Chicago attorney David Fales, described her family's escape: "The fire behind us raged and crackled, and the whole earth, or all we saw of it, was a lurid yellowish red."

After leaping the southern branch of the Chicago River, the fire ignited the waste and oil on the surface of the water. The gasworks exploded, leaving most of the city without lights and further fueling the insatiable flames.

Between 2:00 and 4:00 a.m. the main branch of the Chicago River was breached. The waterworks went up in flames. Residents fled as far east as they could go, to the shoreline of Lake Michigan and into the lake itself, horses and all. To avoid being scorched, they ducked their heads underwater. It didn't always work.

Historians later described The Great Chicago Fire as not one fire but a succession of nine separate fires, each started by flying brands carried on the wind from a previous site. By 6:00 a.m. on Monday, October 9, most of the western portion of the city center was destroyed. The flames also cut a swath across the North Side on their way to the lakefront.

"Chicago is burning!" exclaimed the opening lines of The *Evening Journal-Extra* on October 9. "Up to this hour of writing (1 o'clock p.m.) the best part of the city is already in ashes."

Readers who read the entire article witnessed firsthand the beginning of a legend: "The fire broke out," the paper said, "on the corner of De Koven and Twelfth streets . . . being caused by a cow kicking over a lamp in a stable in which a woman was milking."

This was, as pointed out years later by historian Mabel McIlvaine, "the very first appearance of *The Cow*."

On Monday night, October 9, 1871, rain began to fall.

"On Tuesday morning," wrote William A. Croffut, managing editor of the *Chicago Evening Post,* "the last house burnt, away at the north."

Over on DeKoven Street, Catherine O'Leary bemoaned the loss of her barn, cows, horse, and wagon. She never imagined that she would become a major character in a story that would be carefully passed down through the years into the next century. Upset by the rumors started by the *Evening Journal-Extra,* Catherine and Patrick O'Leary gave sworn statements denying that they were in their barn on the night of October 8 when the fire started. Denis Ryan and Denis Sullivan, another neighbor, also signed affidavits swearing that they roused the O'Learys from bed when the fire started, trying to put an end to the "cow kicked the lantern story."

When all was said and done, the O'Leary home was still standing. The same could not be said for close to three hundred people and more than seventeen thousand buildings within a four-mile radius. The business district and the lakefront harbor no longer existed, nor did a huge chunk of the North Side.

The tragedy inspired John Greenleaf Whittier to write a poem called "Chicago," which contained the verse:

On threescore spires had sunset shone,
Where ghastly sunrise looked on none.
Men clasped each other's hands, and said:
"The City of the West is dead!"

Amazingly, not only was the City of the West not dead, within two years it was completely rebuilt. In physical terms, the new city was far superior to the old one—so much so that Chicago actually celebrated the two-year anniversary of the fire. On that anniversary and each subsequent one for nearly a quarter of a century, reporters came to interview Catherine O'Leary about the cow that kicked over the lantern. She ignored them or chased them away.

A 1938 movie, *In Old Chicago,* helped perpetuate the legend of Mrs. O'Leary and her cow. The story remained largely unchallenged until 1997, when the testimony of historians and an O'Leary descendant caused the city's Committee on Police and Fire to clear the infamous pair—on the 126th anniversary of The Great Fire.

"We always knew that she was innocent," said great-great-granddaughter Nancy Knight Connolly. "But everybody else thought they did it. So now we'll be exonerated."

The Chicago Fire Academy stands on the spot once occupied by the O'Leary barn.

CONFINED AGAINST HER WILL

1875

The woman awoke in a panic, her hand on her chest. At first she could not understand why her heart was pounding so, and then suddenly she knew: Her son was dying.

It didn't matter that he had been in good health the last time she heard from him. She could not shake the overwhelming certainty that he now lay at death's door. Worst of all, he was more than a thousand miles away.

Even though the woman had taken medication to help her sleep, she was wide awake. She hurried to the Western Union office in Jacksonville, Florida, and sent a telegram to her son's law partner that read: "My Belief is my son is ill. Telegraph me at once without a moment's delay—on Receipt of this I start for Chicago."

The woman then sent another telegram to the law partner, this one addressed to her son: "Rouse yourself—and live for my sake. . . . I am praying every moment for your life to be spared."

Death was painfully familiar to the woman. Two of her sons had died when they were children. Ten years ago, her husband had been murdered right in front of her. Just four years ago another son had died at age eighteen. She could not bear the thought of her one remaining son leaving her as the others had. She had to reach him before it was too late.

On a balmy morning in mid-March 1875, the woman put on a black dress and veil—as was her custom since her husband's death— and boarded a train to Chicago. Although her own health problems and brutally cold weather had prompted her to travel south for the winter, Chicago was her home as well as her son's. As the train clattered along the tracks, she chastised herself for going so far away. She would never forgive herself for being absent in her son's hour of need.

When the woman stepped off the train in Chicago, the icy air stung her cheeks. She grabbed hold of her hat to keep the brisk wind from blowing it away. A carriage took her to the Grand Pacific Hotel. There in the lobby was the person she least expected to see.

"Robert!" she cried.

She embraced him. He put an arm around her. Although he was not a tall man, he seemed so next to his mother, who was only five foot two.

"You're not dying," she murmured. "I was so frightened."

Robert assured her that he was fine, as were his wife and children. Everyone was just fine. "Why didn't you wait for my telegram?" he said. "There was no need for you to leave Florida."

The woman sighed. It wasn't the first time Robert had been annoyed with her nor was it likely to be the last. His temperament was so different from his father's. Robert had always been so serious and stuffy. Still, the fact that he was not dying soothed her considerably. She turned her attention to a disturbing incident that had occurred en route to Chicago.

"Robert," she said. "Someone on the train tried to poison me!"

Robert Todd Lincoln took his mother's plump hands in his and listened as patiently as he could. Despite her obvious agitation, he strongly doubted that anyone had tried to poison her. It seemed to him that she was becoming more and more irrational with each passing year. He frowned as he recalled a letter to the editor—signed only with the initial "B"—that had appeared in the *Chicago Tribune*.

"Many who have known Mrs. Lincoln for years, have for a long time unhesitatingly affirmed that her mind was wrecked. The evidences of her insanity, in a thousand ways, are not wanting." The letter-writer further opined that Mary Todd Lincoln's mental problems dated back to her husband Abraham's ascent to the presidency of the United States. In the writer's view, "she had not the moral greatness to bear" such an elevation, and as a result, her mind became "unsettled."

In September 1867, to Robert's profound embarrassment, his mother traveled to New York under a false name. Once there, she attempted to sell her clothing and other personal effects. She couldn't seem to grasp the fact that she was not on the brink of poverty.

And now she had traveled over a thousand miles because she thought he was on his death bed. Nodding absently as his mother continued to prattle about her train ride, Robert escorted her up to her third-floor room at the Grand Pacific. Destroyed in the great fire of 1871, the hotel had reopened just one year later, new and improved, with a domed inner court, a conservatory, and several elevators.

Robert's mother talked him into spending the night in an adjoining room. Before they parted ways, she reassured him that she was taking good care of her money—she had sewn more than $50,000 in government bonds into her petticoats. Appalled, Robert retired to his room, knowing that tomorrow he would have to persuade her to place the bonds elsewhere for safekeeping.

Early the next morning, he was awakened by a shout in the hallway.

"Mrs. Lincoln, you mustn't go down to the lobby like that!"

Robert found his mother standing in front of the elevator half-dressed, a frantic hotel staff member beside her. When Robert placed his hands gently on his mother's shoulders and tried to guide her back to her room, she screamed, "You are going to murder me!" She later explained that she had mistaken the elevator for the bathroom, which was down the hall.

Over the next two months, Mary Todd Lincoln's behavior grew even more troubling. Despite her belief that she was nearly penniless, she paraded from shop to shop in her black gown and widow's veil, spending money lavishly. Clerks tittered nervously at her extravagant purchases: $600 worth of lace curtains, $200 worth of soaps and perfumes, jewelry valued at $700. All the while, Mrs. Lincoln chattered away, revealing details of her personal life in a most unladylike manner. The merchandise was delivered to her hotel room, where it sat unopened.

Robert grew so concerned for her welfare that he hired detectives to follow and watch over her. Her physician, Dr. Willis Danforth, continued to treat her for "nervous derangement and fever in her head," as he had been doing since 1873. He had thought that the milder climate and more leisurely atmosphere in Florida would help relieve her severe, chronic headaches and hallucinations. But he had been wrong.

After consulting with doctors and legal counsel, Robert hired the Chicago firm of Ayer & Kales. They brought in attorney Leonard Swett, an old friend of Abraham Lincoln. Another old family friend, Supreme Court Justice David Davis, firmly believed that Mrs. Lincoln was insane.

"If you don't take action," he warned Robert, "you will bear the responsibility for the disastrous consequences."

In May, Robert learned that his mother was planning a trip to California or possibly Europe. He felt that it would be foolhardy to allow her to travel in her condition. The doctors he had consulted agreed that Mrs. Lincoln was not of sound mind. Reluctantly, Robert set his plan in motion.

Mary Todd Lincoln went shopping on the morning of May 19, 1875. Not long after she returned home, Leonard Swett came to her door. He informed her that she was under arrest and must accompany him to the courthouse, where a jury had been assembled to judge her sanity.

According to Swett, Mrs. Lincoln replied, "I am much obliged to you but I am abundantly able to take care of myself. Where is my son Robert?"

She had no idea that Robert had sworn out the warrant for her arrest as a lunatic, "for her benefit and the safety of the community."

The trial took place in Cook County Courthouse. For three hours, Mrs. Lincoln listened to testimony from doctors, hotel employees, sales clerks, and finally, from Robert himself.

"I have no doubt my mother is insane," he said with tears in his eyes. "She has long been a source of great anxiety to me."

The defense lawyer, handpicked by Robert, did not contest the case or call any witnesses. The jury took ten minutes to determine "that Mary Lincoln is insane and is a fit person to be in a state hospital for the insane."

Mrs. Lincoln spent four months at Bellevue Place, a small, private sanatorium in Batavia, Illinois. She then moved to Springfield, to the home of her sister and brother-in-law, Elizabeth and Ninian Edwards—the same house in which she had married Abraham Lincoln. Nine months later, a second insanity hearing in Chicago determined that Mrs. Lincoln was "restored to reason and capable to manage and control her estate."

Mary Todd Lincoln died on July 16, 1882. Some say that she never forgave Robert for having her confined against her will at Bellevue Place. Others say that mother and son reconciled in 1881. To this day, historians continue to explore and examine the extent of Mrs. Lincoln's insanity and Robert's motives.

ATROCIOUS ACTS

1886

"Tuesday night came, warm and damp," wrote Paul C. Hull, *Chicago Daily News* reporter and eyewitness. "It was dark and starless, and across the somber sky black clouds scudded. With the falling darkness came rugged and roughly dressed men to Haymarket square."

Hull's theatrical prose was the style of the day, but given what happened on May 4, 1886, a simple recitation of the facts would have been dramatic enough.

That night, about twenty-five hundred people gathered at Haymarket Square, an open area two blocks long on Randolph Street between Des Plaines and Halsted Streets. They came in response to a handbill announcing a "Great Mass Meeting." The circular promised "Good speakers will be present to denounce the latest atrocious act of the police."

The "atrocious act" mentioned in the handbill was one of a long series of atrocious acts committed by labor activists and police all across America. Over the past decade, acts of violence had created an atmosphere of distrust, animosity, and fear.

On May 1, 1886, one hundred thousand American workers went on strike in support of the eight-hour workday. At first, demonstrations in Chicago were peaceful. However, on May 3, strikers attacked replacement workers as they left McCormick's Reaper Works. The police responded with guns and clubs, killing six strikers.

August Spies, editor for the *Arbeiter-Zeitung,* an anarchist newspaper, expressed his outrage in a broadsheet. "Workingmen to Arms!" it read. "Your masters sent out their bloodhounds the police. They killed six of your brothers at McCormick's this afternoon."

Attendance at the May 4 "Mass Meeting" at Haymarket Square was far lower than organizers had hoped it would be. Spies moved the gathering up Des Plaines Street to an area near the mouth of an alley. He climbed onto an empty truck wagon and addressed the group. "There seems to prevail the opinion in certain quarters that this meeting has been called for the purpose of inaugurating a riot."

By "certain quarters" he meant the Chicago police. About half a block away, at the Des Plaines Street station, close to one hundred and eighty officers were on standby. According to reporter Hull, they were armed with extra-long hickory clubs and forty-eight-caliber revolvers. They awaited orders from their commander, Inspector John Bonfield—nicknamed "Black Jack" for his brutal suppression of a trolley strike the previous year.

At around 8:30 p.m., Mayor Carter Harrison arrived at the station. When asked if he intended to prevent the gathering, he replied, "I have no right to interfere with any peaceable meeting of the people. Should the crowd become troublesome, I will disperse it."

Less than one hundred yards away, Spies continued his speech. "The object of this meeting is to explain the general situation of the eight-hour movement and to throw light upon various incidents in connection with it."

Mayor Harrison stopped by the rally to assess the mood of the crowd. He listened to Spies and then to another speaker. Deeming their rhetoric milder than usual, he departed. On his way home, he met with Inspector Bonfield at the Des Plaines station and suggested that he dismiss the reserves.

The wind and drizzle began to take its toll on the audience. Hundreds left before Samuel Fielden, a stonemason and known labor orator, started his speech at 10:00 p.m. A few minutes later, Hull reported, "there suddenly came from the north an icy wind. . . . With it came rolling rapidly up a huge black cloud, which threatened to burst into a storm."

More people left, though an estimated three hundred remained to hear the rest of Fielden's speech. As the rain fell harder, his tone grew harsher and his language more forceful.

"A million men hold all the property in this country. The law has no use for the other fifty-four millions. You have nothing more to do with the law except to lay hands on it and throttle it until it makes its last kick."

Disturbed by the speech and by the crowd, which seemed to grow noisier, the plainclothes detectives assigned by Bonfield to monitor the meeting reported their impressions to the inspector. He still had the full contingent of police at his command.

On Bonfield's orders the officers formed two columns and marched up Des Plaines Street. Hull mounted an iron stairway to get a good view. The police stopped a few feet from the speakers' wagon. Captain William Ward called out, "I command you, in the name of the people of the state of Illinois, immediately and peaceably to disperse!"

"But we are peaceable," Fielden protested.

The captain repeated his command.

"All right, we will go," responded Fielden, stepping down from the wagon.

Suddenly, a sputtering, hissing spark of fire arched through the air and fell into the midst of the police. A deafening explosion shook the street, shattering windows.

"I saw the second and third companies of police fall to the ground as one man," Hull wrote.

For a few seconds, there was absolute silence. Then the shooting began.

Fearing the police would fire high to disperse the crowd, Hull rushed down to the street. "At the first step a man in front of me was shot," he reported, "I fell over him. At the same instant a man behind me was shot. He fell on my shoulders and head. The bullets buzzed like bees, and the clubs cracked on human skulls. I expected every instant to feel a bullet in my flesh."

Within five minutes it was over. Doctors, nurses, and priests arrived as quickly as horses could carry them. They were too late to help Patrolman Mathias Degan, who died when bomb fragments severed his artery.

Six of the wounded officers died in the ten days that followed the bombing. About fifty others survived. Although some of the civilians at the meeting were armed, many of the injured policemen were hit by "friendly fire."

Four civilian deaths were recorded. Many victims who sought treatment for their wounds refused to give their names. An accurate count was impossible.

In subsequent days, police stormed through the city arresting thousands of known or suspected anarchists. The business community, the police, and the mainstream press insisted that the anarchists had conspired to kill policemen. Anarchist organizations charged that the entire incident was prearranged by industrialists and police.

On June 21, eight men went on trial as accessories before the fact in the murder of Mathias Degan. They were Albert Parsons, August

Spies, Samuel Fielden, George Engel, Louis Lingg, Adolph Fischer, Oscar Neebe, and Michael Schwab. Rudolph Schnaubelt had been indicted as the bomb thrower, but he fled the city before the trial. His guilt was never proven, and he was never apprehended.

The jury delivered its verdict on August 20. They found the defendants guilty of murder and fixed the penalty at death for all but Oscar Neebe, who was sentenced to fifteen years in the penitentiary. As presiding judge Joseph Gary put it, the defendants "incited, advised, encouraged the throwing of the bomb that killed the policemen . . . by general addresses to readers and hearers."

Appeals to the Illinois Supreme Court and the U.S. Supreme Court failed. On November 10, Governor Richard J. Oglesby commuted the death sentences of Samuel Fielden and Michael Schwab, who had officially asked for mercy. Louis Lingg committed suicide in his cell.

In spite of petitions for clemency signed by thousands of citizens, the four remaining defendants—Parsons, Spies, Engel, and Fischer—were executed November 11, 1886. Nearly two hundred witnesses observed the hanging.

In June 1893, Governor John Peter Altgeld pardoned Fielden, Neebe, and Schwab. His reasons, among others, were that the jury was "packed" (selected to convict) and "the trial judge was either so prejudiced against the defendants, or else so determined to win the applause of a certain class in the community that he could not and did not grant a fair trial." For his trouble, Altgeld was accused in newspapers all across the country of being an anarchist himself.

Historians consider Haymarket one of the seminal events in the history of American labor. As Robert G. Spinney put it, the Haymarket bombing "highlighted deep anxieties regarding labor radicalism, urban unrest, safety, and law and order." The tragedy won many converts to anarchism. However, it also impeded the eight-hour day movement and the efforts of organized labor in general.

A GENUINE REFUGE

1890

The big, old house on Halsted Street had seen better days. Built in 1856, it was originally a "country home," shaded by majestic trees and encircled by a well-kept lawn. Now, thirty-four years later, it was crammed between a mortuary and a saloon in Chicago's Nineteenth Ward, one of the city's poorest, most crowded neighborhoods.

None of that mattered to the panicked girl who darted across the wide veranda late one afternoon. She burst through the front door into the large, handsomely decorated reception area.

"Help!" she cried. "Somebody help!"

A small, frail-looking young woman rose from her chair in alarm. "What is it? What is wrong?"

"This girl who lives in our house, she's hollerin' somethin' fierce! My mother says it's disgracin' the whole house!"

"Why is she hollering?"

"She's havin' a baby!"

Another young woman entered the reception room to see what the commotion was about. Like the first woman, she was dressed very fashionably, in a white blouse and long, dark skirt. "Won't any-one in your building help her?" she asked the girl.

"She ain't married," the girl said. "They say they'll not touch the likes of her. And they won't call a doctor 'cause she don't have no money. They're afraid he'll want them to pay for it."

The two women exchanged worried glances. Although both were college-educated and highly intelligent, neither was trained as a midwife.

"Where is the poor girl's mother?" one of them asked.

"She does laundry over on the north side, but nobody knows the address. Please, you got to come! She just keeps yellin'."

Jane Addams and Julia Lathrop looked at each other again. This was not the sort of service they were prepared to provide at Hull-House. The facility offered child care, as well as classes in sewing, dancing, cooking, history, languages, mathematics, and literature. Delivering babies was not on the program, but the two women could not imagine turning the frantic girl away.

"There seemed nothing for it but to go ourselves," Addams wrote years later, "and Julia Lathrop and I set forth leaving a resident at the telephone calling up a friendly neighborhood doctor."

They hurried along the wooden planks that served as a sidewalk, past saloons and shops, past a peddler's horse-drawn wagon filled with junk.

"We found the poor girl alone in her agony," Addams recalled, "and by the time the doctor finally arrived, almost at the very moment that the girl's mother returned from her work, the patient was lying in a clean bed and the baby, having been induced to cry lustily, was having his first bath."

Mother and daughter were so grateful to the two women who answered the cry for help, they named the baby boy Julius John in their honor.

On the way home, Addams exclaimed to Lathrop, "This doing things that we don't know how to do is going too far. Why did we let ourselves be rushed into midwifery?"

"To refuse to respond to a poor girl in the throes of childbirth would be a disgrace to us forevermore," Lathrop replied. "If Hull-House does not have its roots in human kindness, it is no good at all."

Sadly, human kindness could not keep Julius John from dying at the age of four months. In the late 1800s, it was not uncommon for infants to die in Chicago's Nineteenth Ward, nor was it surprising, given the conditions.

Located on Chicago's Near West Side, the Nineteenth Ward was bounded by Polk Street on the north, Twelfth Street on the south, and State Street on the east. Most of the people who lived there were immigrants who had come to America from Italy, Poland, Russia, Ireland, Bohemia, Greece, and Germany.

Jane Addams wrote: "The streets are inexpressibly dirty . . . sanitary legislation unenforced . . . and the stables foul beyond description. Hundreds of houses are unconnected with the street sewer."

The Nineteenth Ward was the heart of Chicago's garment industry, which employed a great number of the immigrants. Children age fourteen and older were legally permitted to work. Regardless of age, factory employees typically worked ten hours a day, six days a week. They were allowed half an hour for lunch, which they usually ate at their work stations.

Children played in rat-infested alleys. The streets were paved with wooden blocks. When it rained heavily, the blocks came loose and floated about. Foul-smelling standing water remained for days.

These deplorable conditions were the very reason Jane Addams and her friend Ellen Gates Starr decided to move to the area in 1889. Inspired by a visit to Toynbee Hall, a pioneering social settlement in

London, Addams and Starr wanted to provide a place where socially conscious young women could share their knowledge with people who otherwise might not have opportunities to enrich and improve their lives.

On the first day of their search, Addams and Starr were delighted to discover the former residence of real estate developer and philanthropist Charles J. Hull. The mansion on South Halsted Street was in rough shape, but its stately Corinthian columns and arched windows gave it a dignified air.

They moved in on September 18, 1889, furnishing the house at their own expense. Joining them was Mary Keyser, whose initial position was that of housekeeper. Keyser's role expanded quickly, and she become known for her "neighborly work," described by one reporter as "the visiting of the sick, the daily ministration to the needy and heartsick and the despairing."

By the time Julia Lathrop came to live at Hull-House, it had a full program of activities, including a kindergarten every day from 9:00 a.m. until noon. Thursday afternoons, a female doctor provided advice to neighborhood women. Social receptions were held regularly, often geared toward specific ethnic groups. Lathrop immediately started a Plato Club, which met Sundays at 4:00 p.m. University of Chicago student John Dewey, who became a well-known philosopher and educator, often led the discussion.

Addams was not surprised by the high level of participation from the area's residents. In her book *Twenty Years at Hull-House,* she explained why:

> *Men and women of education and refinement come to*
> *live in a cheaper neighborhood because they lack the*
> *ability to make money, because of ill health, because of*
> *an unfortunate marriage, or for other reasons which*

do not imply criminality or stupidity. . . . To such the Settlement may be a genuine refuge.

Addams noted that the most popular type of class was "a combination of a social atmosphere with serious study." Among the guest lecturers were suffragist Susan B. Anthony, attorney Clarence Darrow, and architect Frank Lloyd Wright.

As Hull-House expanded, its reputation grew. Writing in 1891, reporter Jeannette L. Gilder of New York declared: "Hull House . . . might well be copied by the philanthropically inclined of New York. . . . At present, Chicago is ahead of us."

Just as Toynbee Hall inspired Addams and Starr, Hull-House inspired the establishment of settlements all over America. Hull-House itself grew into a thirteen-building complex that enveloped the original building. Among the additions made over the years were an art gallery, apartment buildings, and a nursery.

Jane Addams became famous for her work at Hull-House as well as her role in many local and national organizations. In 1931, she received the Nobel Peace Prize. Julia Lathrop, who accompanied Addams on many an errand of mercy, aided in founding Cook County Juvenile Court, the first juvenile court in the world. Hull-House ended its role as a settlement house in 1963. All but two of the thirteen buildings were torn down to make room for the University of Illinois at Chicago campus. The original building on South Halsted Street now contains Hull-House Museum. The Jane Addams Hull House Association carries on the work begun by its founder, providing programs for underserved communities in and around Chicago and advocating for public policy reforms.

"THE VERY ESSENCE
OF AMERICAN PROGRESS"

1893

In the early 1880s, momentum began building for a World's Fair commemorating the four hundredth anniversary of Columbus's voyage to the New World. During the Gilded Age, World's Fairs were relatively commonplace. London held the first one—the Crystal Palace Exhibition—in 1851. Other major cities followed suit. There was much competition to see what city would host the Columbian Exposition.

An editorial cartoon published in New York in August 1889 satirized the situation. In the cartoon, several women gather around Uncle Sam, waiting to see which one will receive the bouquet in his hands. All the ladies are beautiful and elegantly dressed except one: a bony, homely girl wearing an evening gown covered with a pattern of little pigs. Huge, gaudy diamonds embellish her bust and drip from her ears. She stretches out her skinny arms, her mouth open as if demanding the bouquet. One of the stylish society women glares at her with contempt.

The bouquet represented the World's Fair. The fashionable ladies were the great cities of America (New York, Washington, D.C., and St. Louis), vying for the privilege of hosting the Fair. The uncouth girl was labeled "Chicago." The pig motif on the girl's gown referred to Chicago's dominant role in the meatpacking industry.

Chicago was more than half a century old at the time, having been founded in 1833. However, the Great Fire had destroyed much of the town in 1871. Thus, it could be asserted that the city reborn from the ashes was just eighteen. The notion of The Prairie City hosting a World's Fair was viewed as both preposterous and appalling.

On August 10, 1889 the *New York Times* announced smugly:

> *An epidemic of typhoid fever prevails in the southern part of Chicago, owing to the pollution of the city's supply of water by the sewage that flows into the lake from which the water is taken. We suggest that some of the energy now being expended by the people of Chicago in an effort to procure the World's Fair for their city might well be used in obtaining a supply of clean water.*

Health concerns aside, New York sophisticates also warned that Chicago would embarrass the entire country by staging a World's Fair that was little more than a cattle show. They found Chicago's barefaced enthusiasm and strident self-promotion unseemly.

"In this as in many of its public endeavors," sniffed the *New York Times,* "the methods of Chicago are noisy and more or less offensive to dignity and good taste."

Undeterred, Chicago's supporters continued to offer reasons why Chicago was at least as good a choice as any other city in the running.

"Columbus did not discover New York, Washington, or St. Louis any more than he did Chicago," asserted World's Fair committee member Robert Lindblom, who hailed from Sweden. "He did not even discover North America at all except theoretically."

Full-page advertising supplements appeared in *Harper's Weekly* magazine. Titled "Chicago: The Best Location for The World's Exposition of 1892," the ads featured Chicago's most impressive buildings and lengthy descriptions of the city's advantages, not the least of which was its position as a transportation hub.

It soon became known that the U.S. Congress would choose the location of the World's Fair based primarily on financial resources. New Yorkers were stunned when they realized, near the end of 1889, that the competition had been reduced to two candidates: New York and Chicago.

As late as January 15, 1890, New York was still convinced that it would win. "New York Feels Confident," read the headline in the *New York Times*. "Sure Now That The World's Fair Will Be Held Here."

As the saying goes, "It isn't over until it's over," or in this case, "It isn't over until the girl in the pig-print dress plunks down her last dollar." Thanks to banker Lyman Gage's fund-raising ability, The Prairie City plunked down several million "last dollars" in a twenty-four-hour period, thereby trumping New York's final offer. Gage's efforts put the icing on the cake so lovingly prepared by such Chicago notables as Charles T. Yerkes, Marshall Field, Philip Armour, Potter Palmer, Gustavus Swift, George Pullman, Cyrus McCormick, and tens of thousands of Chicagoans who bought subscriptions.

On March 19 the *New York Times* printed an announcement that must have made its editors grind their teeth: "The World's Fair

Committee of the House held what will probably be its last meeting this morning. The result of the session was a complete victory for the Chicago people." In April President Benjamin Harrison signed a bill officially naming Chicago the host city.

The World's Columbian Exposition quickly began to take shape under the direction of Colonel George Royal Davis, U.S. Representative from Illinois. Davis, who had helped plead Chicago's case in Congress, described the city as "the very essence of American progress . . . essentially the most distinctively American of the great towns of the United States." Chicago was, he declared, the most appropriate host for a "celebration of our four centuries of unexampled prosperity."

The site chosen for the Fair was Jackson Park, a marshy area on Lake Michigan about seven miles south of the Loop. Dredging and filling started in the early winter of 1891. Over a period of many months, workers transformed swamp and sand hill into grand basins and broad lagoons, intermingled with parks containing more than a million transplanted trees, bushes, and plants.

Construction of buildings began in the spring of 1892. In early June, the *Chicago Tribune* reported that "an average of 6,016 men have been employed at Jackson Park during the month of May. . . . Nine State buildings and one foreign building are under way."

People considered the Fair a great entertainment value even before it opened. Thousands of visitors paid a fee to watch the process. For workers, inclement weather and pressure to meet their deadline combined to create conditions that were not entertaining in the least. During the twenty-month construction period, more than seven hundred accidents and eighteen deaths occurred, despite stringent safety precautions.

The World's Columbian Exposition opened on May 1, 1893. To create a sense of unity, the fourteen main exposition buildings were all designed in Beaux-Arts style. Buildings in the Court of Honor surrounding the Grand Basin were covered with plaster of Paris and painted white, prompting people to refer to the entire complex as the "White City."

In addition to the stunning architecture and sixty-five thousand exhibits, the Exposition boasted an amusement park called the Midway. It was there that visitors encountered the first Ferris wheel, an astonishing contraption invented by thirty-two-year-old engineer George W. Ferris. Mounted on the wheel were three thousand of Thomas Edison's new incandescent light bulbs, blinking on and off.

The Fair also introduced visitors to new products such as Cracker Jacks, Juicy Fruit gum, Pabst beer, and Cream of Wheat. Statistics show that approximately 25 percent of the population of the United States visited the Fair before it closed its gates on October 31, 1893.

Historians view the World's Columbian Exposition as an example of the confidence and optimism that pervaded America near the end of the nineteenth century. Feelings of national pride were dealt a harsh blow near the end of the Fair, when Mayor Carter Harrison was assassinated. Bright hopes were further challenged by a severe economic depression that began that same year.

Only history can judge how well the Fair met its official goals: to provide stability in the face of great change, to encourage American unity, to celebrate technology and commerce, and to encourage popular education. The Exposition proved one thing for certain. The girl in the pig-print dress had every right to hold her head high in the presence of the country's grand dames. Chicago had come of age.

"SEWED UP HIS HEART"

1893

Wednesday, July 9, 1893, started out as a typical day for James Cornish. The twenty-four-year-old man reported as usual to the main office of the delivery service that employed him. The oppressive heat and humidity made the day seem extra long. By evening, he was more than ready for a cold drink.

At his favorite saloon on Chicago's South side, people were joking, drinking, and playing cards. Some were talking about "The White City"—the World's Fair that had opened in May. Cornish ordered a whiskey from the bartender and joined a couple of his friends at the poker table. Somebody put a coin in the player piano in the corner, and the notes of the song "Daisy Bell" rolled through the smoke-filled air.

Nobody knew exactly how the fight started. One minute there was music and laughter and the sound of cards being shuffled. The next minute, a chair slammed against the bar with a crash, a table tipped over, and fists began to fly.

"He's got a knife!" a man yelled.

Cornish turned in the direction of the voice and collided with someone. Suddenly a sharp, ice-cold pain shot through his body. He gasped and clutched his chest. His knees buckled. He went down.

Just up the road, at 29th and Dearborn Streets, Dr. Daniel Hale Williams was deep in conversation with a colleague. The narrow, three-story brick house in which the doctors stood had opened its doors two years ago as a twelve-bed hospital and nurse-training facility. It was the only facility in Chicago—and one of the first in the nation—to train and employ African-American interns and nurses. It was also one of the few to offer full hospital privileges to African-American physicians.

Provident Hospital, as it was called, was committed to serving the poor of all races. The generosity of prominent citizens and dedicated community members had made it possible for Provident to pursue its lofty mission. Donors included the great African-American leader and orator Frederick Douglass, a distant kinsman of Dr. Williams. However, Provident still lacked basic equipment, and making ends meet was a never-ending struggle.

As chief of staff, Dr. Williams insisted on the highest clinical standards and rigorous attention to hygiene throughout the facility. Even so, he knew Provident couldn't compare with larger institutions like Mercy Hospital, where he had interned in the early 1880s. At Provident, the "emergency room" was a small space in the rear of the building. Although it was plain and cramped, it was exactly what James Cornish needed on the evening of July 9, 1893.

Dr. Williams took one look at the blood gushing from Cornish's chest and shouted for assistance. Closer examination revealed that the wound was just to the left of the sternum, or breastbone, and about one inch long. Dr. Williams probed the wound superficially, and then admitted Cornish to the hospital for observation. During the night, Cornish experienced excessive bleeding, pain over the area of the heart, and symptoms of shock.

The morning of July 10, Dr. Williams determined that the knife had penetrated far enough to wound Cornish's internal mammary artery and veins. If he wanted to try to save Cornish's life, he was going to have to open his chest and repair the damage. The decision to do so could not be made lightly. In 1893, every physician knew that internal operations were extremely dangerous. The chance of infection was high no matter how careful and meticulous the technique. Death was common. Surgery in the area of the heart was deemed particularly hazardous. Doctors believed that even simple manipulation of the heart might cause lethal disturbances.

The risks were duly noted, yet to Dr. Williams and the five other doctors who joined him that morning, it was apparent that without an operation, James Cornish would probably die from his injury. They prepared to perform surgery in the converted bedroom that served as Provident's operating room.

From a modern perspective, the list of medical aids *not* available at the time is sobering: There were no X-rays, no artificial airway to keep the windpipe open, no blood transfusions, no penicillin or other antibiotics, no powerful intravenous anesthetics. Administration of anesthesia primarily involved guesswork.

In a report published in 1897, Dr. Williams described the initial steps of the operation on James Cornish:

> *[The] wound was lengthened to the right, second incision was made from the centre of the first, carried over the middle of the cartilage and fifth rib about six inches in length. Sternum, cartilage, and about one inch of the fifth rib were exposed. Cartilage of the fifth rib was separated at its junction with the sternum.*

Peering through an entrance about the size of a knothole, the doctor could see a laceration in the pericardium (the membranous sac that holds the heart). He also noticed a puncture wound about one-tenth of an inch long in the myocardium (the muscular tissue of the heart itself). Dr. Williams decided that the heart muscle did not need to be sutured. The pericardial wound was a different matter.

After irrigating the wound with normal salt solution, Dr. Williams grasped the edges with forceps and stitched the wound shut. All the while, Cornish's heart continued to beat within the sac. Dr. Williams closed the incisions, and a dry dressing was applied to the site.

On July 22, 1893, the *Daily Inter Ocean* ran a headline guaranteed to stop people in their tracks: "SEWED UP HIS HEART." In the style of the day, several subheads followed: "Remarkable Surgical Operation . . . At Provident Hospital . . . A Puncture in the Vital Organ Exposed and Dressed with Success." The article made the most of an opportunity to praise Dr. Williams and his work:

> *Three-fourths of the cases treated in this institution are*
> *of the surgical class. Dr. Williams, the chief surgeon,*
> *said yesterday that he and his assistants were sometimes*
> *called on to perform difficult operations which would*
> *not have been attempted in any hospital ten years ago,*
> *and success crowned their efforts in almost every case.*

Cornish remained in stable condition for eighteen days. Then, on August 2, Dr. Williams had to make another incision in order to remove excess fluid from around the lungs. This development was not unexpected. Again, Dr. Williams's rigorous attention to maintaining sterile conditions helped prevent infection.

"Following this operation there was nothing worthy of note," he wrote in his report. "The patient left the hospital well, August 30th."

Cornish did so well that he quickly returned to his normal activities. Several months after being released from the hospital, he showed up again, hollering for "Dr. Dan." It wasn't a social call. Cornish had been in another fight, and his head was covered in blood.

"I got to see Dr. Dan!" he yelled.

According to Jessie Sleet Scales, a nurse who witnessed the event, Dr. Williams pretended to be doubtful that Cornish was worth saving. Cornish howled louder than ever. Dr. Williams finally said: "Well, you have got some nice fancy work in you, Cornish. I guess I can't afford to lose you. You're an important specimen." A week later, after his stitches were removed, Cornish was released again.

In 1897, the journal *Medical Record* published Dr. Williams's report describing the surgery on Cornish's heart. Almost from that very moment, controversy ensued over whether Dr. Williams performed "the first successful heart surgery." The argument can and has been made that operating on the pericardium does not qualify as heart surgery. It has also been stated that Dr. Williams was not the first to operate on the pericardium.

Whether one believes that Daniel Hale Williams has received more—or less—credit than he deserves, certain things are incontestable: Daniel Hale Williams was a highly skilled, successful pioneer in the field of cardiovascular surgery, a notable champion in the effort to bring African Americans into the medical professions, and a key participant in the fight to provide quality health care to people of all races and income levels.

Not only was Dr. Williams instrumental in the establishment of Provident Hospital, he served on the staffs of other Chicago hospitals as well as Freedmen's Hospital in Washington, D.C. He was professor of clinical surgery at Meharry Medical College in Nashville, Tennessee, and a member of the Illinois State Board of Health. In 1913, he became the only African-American charter member of the American College of Surgeons. Dr. Williams passed away in 1931. His "important specimen," James Cornish, outlived him by twelve years.

THE RACE OF THE CENTURY

1895

Herman H. Kohlsaat, publisher of the *Chicago Times-Herald,* pushed his chair back from his table at the Chicago Club. In his hand he held a copy of the French magazine *L'Illustration,* containing information about a race from Paris to Bordeaux. The competitors would not race on foot, horseback, or bicycle—although those kinds of races were popular in 1895. Instead, they would race in contraptions that had no "official" name. The French called them *automobiles.*

By the time Kohlsaat got back to his office, he knew he wanted to host a race in Chicago. Years later in an article for the *Saturday Evening Post,* he wrote: "The *Times-Herald* offered five thousand dollars in prizes. The race was to be run July 4, 1895. Some sixty contestants entered the lists."

Each vehicle in the contest had to have at least three wheels and be able to carry at least two people. One of these people would be an umpire selected by the judges. In order to qualify, entrants had to have their vehicles tested in areas such as fuel consumption, load capacity, and tractability. Kohlsaat wanted the contest to be more about the capability and practicality of horseless carriages in general than about winning a race.

"There was considerable opposition to calling the horseless carriage 'automobile,'" Kohlsaat wrote, "as the name was too Frenchy, so the *Times-Herald* offered five hundred dollars for a name, and 'motocycle' was awarded the prize."

"When July Fourth arrived there was only one machine ready," Kohlsaat noted later. "As it was impossible to have a contest with one machine, the time was extended to Labor Day, in September."

On July 9, Kohlsaat's paper ran an article on page 1 titled "Prize for Motors . . . Cash Reward for Inventors . . . Three Sums of Money for Men Who Can Construct Practicable, Self-Propelling Road Carriages." The article hastened to reassure readers: "This offer is made with no idea or intention of starting a 'horseless carriage fad,' or of promoting a craze in this direction."

When Kohlsaat was asked to reschedule again, he settled on Thanksgiving Day, November 28, 1895.

In the interim, newspapers all across the country printed editorials about the pros and cons of "carriages propelled by motors." In July 1895, the *Chicago Daily Tribune* noted that the horseless carriage had been seen in Paris for some years already. "Perhaps one reason for this is the exceptional pavements the gay city enjoys," the newspaper opined.

The *Times-Herald* declared that the route planned for the race—Chicago to Milwaukee—probably offered "as fine a roadway for such a test as can be found in this country." The article continued: "There are no hills of too steep a grade and in ordinary weather the entire distance is favored with roads which are the delight of bicycle riders."

The phrase "in ordinary weather" was not printed in bold type or italicized for emphasis, but perhaps it should have been. Winter came early to Chicago in 1895 with a blizzard that hit the city on

November 26. The sun melted the top layer of snow on November 27, and it froze that night. The day of the Big Race, twelve inches of snow lay on the ground, covered by a frozen crust.

One onlooker described conditions:

That frozen crust carried men and sleighs on Thursday morning. Horses and autos broke thru. By noon it began to soften. Was slushy by dark when it began to rain a little. The snow dumped into streets from roofs and walks made them indescribable!

The route was shortened from the original plan. The new course was from the World's Fair German Building in Jackson Park to Evanston and back, a distance of 53.5 miles. The World's Fair (held two years earlier) highlighted several new forms of transportation, including cable cars, elevated trains, and electric trolleys.

Contestants for the race came to Chicago from as far away as New York, Pennsylvania, Connecticut, and Massachusetts and from as close as Decatur, Illinois. One entrant was from Chicago itself. The evening before the race, eleven of the original sixty-odd entrants declared their intent to participate. Five broke down on their way to the starting point, leaving a field of six at the post:

- Duryea Wagon Motor Company of Springfield, Massachusetts (gasoline; manufactured by Duryea of Massachusetts)

- De La Vergne Refrigerator Machine Company of New York (gasoline; manufactured by Benz of Germany)

- Morris and Salom of Philadelphia (the Electrobat II, electric, built by Henry Morris and Pedro Salom)

- H. Mueller & Co. of Decatur (gasoline; manufactured by Benz of Germany)

- R. H. Macy of New York (gasoline; manufactured by Benz of Germany)

- Sturges Electric Motorcycle of Chicago (electric; built by William Morrison of Iowa)

About sixty people showed up in Jackson Park for the start of the race. Kohlsaat and Adams had envisioned hundreds of spectators. However, the weather deterred many, and a Thanksgiving Day football game between the University of Michigan and the University of Chicago drew approximately ten thousand fans, some of whom might otherwise have gone to the race.

Because the contest was designed more to test endurance than speed, entrants' starting times were staggered in order to prevent accidents. At 8:55 a.m. the Duryea wagon, the only American gasoline entry and a strong favorite, pulled away from the starting line with Frank Duryea at the wheel. His umpire was Arthur W. White, a newspaper man from Toronto. The rest of the competitors followed at brief intervals.

Both of the electric machines broke down before they got out of Jackson Park. They had not been considered serious contenders anyway because their owners had no way of recharging along the route. The De La Vergne Benz car got stuck in the snow on Michigan Boulevard, and its owners withdrew from the race.

The Duryea car had to be repaired due to a steering malfunction, allowing the Macy Benz to hold a slight lead approaching the turnaround point at Evanston. However, the Duryea machine soon overtook the Macy vehicle and passed it. The two wagons seemed destined to create a photo finish until the Macy Benz challenged a horse-drawn carriage for the right of way and lost. The steering gear and four wheel spokes on the Benz were bent, and the wheels themselves were damaged. The Macy machine never recovered.

All along the route, contestants dodged snowballs thrown by energetic boys. Most of the cars had no brakes, which made it difficult to avoid collisions with non-motorized carriages whose drivers refused to yield to an apparatus they felt did not belong on the road. Participants forged ahead with little food, no rest, and no heat. The hour grew late. Darkness loomed. At Jackson Park, people checked their watches, shook their heads, and headed home.

Just before 6:00 p.m., the Duryea machine entered Douglas Park. The men onboard began to whoop and shout as they headed down the home stretch. A few people here and there waved and either cheered or jeered. At 7:18 p.m., Duryea crossed the finish line. The Mueller Benz, limping slightly from injuries to its high-speed clutch, arrived at about 8:58 p.m. In the driver's seat was umpire Charles King. Mueller had passed out. No one else completed the race.

The *Chicago Daily Tribune,* refusing to offer even the slightest praise for a contest sponsored by a rival paper, noted:

> *The time of the winner was 10:17 for the fifty-five
> miles. No records, but various parts of the mechanism,
> were broken. . . . Meanwhile the judges had become
> disgusted and quit and no one witnessed the finish but
> two reporters.*

Times-Herald reporter Frederick Adams admitted:

> *Not fifty people saw the last stages of the finish, or
> knew that the Duryea had established a world's record*

*in the capacity of a motocycle to conquer even King
Winter himself.*

Arthur White, the umpire riding shotgun on the Duryea
machine, offered additional details in his report: "Our correct time
was seven hours and fifty-three minutes. We covered a distance of
54.36 miles—averaging a little more than seven miles per hour."

The judges awarded Duryea the $2,000 prize. The Mueller car
received $1,500. The Sturges-Morrison and Macy machines earned
$500 each for the impressive showing they made in the race. Cash
awards were also given for various aspects of vehicle design. Every car that
left the starting point received recognition of some sort from the judges.

Not long after the race, the American Motor League, the world's
first automobile association, was formed. Although the horseless
carriage was known by many names in its formative years—motor
wagon, buggyaut, motor carriage, motorig, and autometon—eventually one name replaced all of them. It combined the Greek word
auto (self) and the Latin word *mobilis* (moving).

Inspired by the Chicago race, E. P. Ingersoll, founder and editor
of the *Horseless Age* magazine predicted a glowing future for the automobile: "In cities and in towns the noise and clatter of the streets will
be reduced," he wrote. "Streets will be cleaner, jams and blockades
less likely to occur, and accidents less frequent, for the horse is not
so manageable as a mechanical vehicle."

In August 1897, the *New York Times* reported that "the new
mechanical wagon with the awful name automobile . . . has come to
stay." The newspaper then drew a conclusion that we might dispute
today: "Man loves the horse, and he is not likely ever to love the
automobile."

THE FALL OF THE SAUSAGE KING

1897

On September 8, 1897, Chicago languished in the throes of a heat wave. In spite of the unbearable weather, Adolph Ludwig Luetgert was in fine form. Broad-shouldered and heavyset, he tilted back in his chair, legs crossed. His five-foot ten-inch frame was stretched out in a relaxed pose. Between puffs on a cigar, he regaled his visitors with witty observations.

Born in Germany in 1845, Luetgert had come to America at age twenty-four. A few years later, he started a sausage-manufacturing company in Chicago. Ambitious and hardworking, he became a prominent member of the city's German community. People began to refer to him as "The Sausage King." Next door to his brick and stone factory, he built a handsome, three-story wooden house.

Luetgert was at his best when he had an audience. He laughed loudly and often, usually at his own jokes. Occasionally he smoothed his bushy moustache or ran a hand through his thick hair. To the people gathered around him in September 1897, he quipped:

"Smoking and walking and eating and sleeping take up my time. I'm not nervous. Why should I be?"

His visitors glanced at each other, eyebrows raised. They could think of several reasons why Luetgert should be nervous. Earlier that year, he had lost a huge sum of money to a con artist. The bank had foreclosed on his factory. And that was the least of Luetgert's problems. Although he behaved as if he were entertaining guests in his parlor, he was actually imprisoned in the Cook County Jail, charged with murdering his wife. She had gone missing more than four months earlier, on May 1.

State's Attorney Charles S. Deneen was trying to get a jury to convict Luetgert of murder even though Louise Luetgert's body had not been found. Luetgert seemed certain he would be acquitted. One of his jailers commented, "He is the most remarkable character that has ever come under my observation. Nothing seems to worry him. He eats regularly and sleeps like a child. I can't fathom him."

Mrs. Luetgert, born Louise (or Louisa) Bicknese in Germany in 1855, had immigrated to America at age seventeen with her brother Diedrich. They arrived in New York in 1872. Louise met Luetgert in Chicago, and they were married in 1878. At the time of Mrs. Luetgert's disappearance, a sister, Wilhelmina Mueller, also lived in Chicago. Diedrich Bicknese lived on a farm in nearby Wood Dale.

Adolph Luetgert said his wife left him because of his business troubles and he had no idea where she was. Newspapers picked up his version of the story and ran with it. On May 9, under the headline "Husband's Reverses Said to Have Preyed on Mrs. Luetgert," the *Chicago Daily Tribune* asserted, "Her husband and three children are anxiously hoping for news that will give them assurance of her safety." The "three children" consisted of Louis and Elmer (born to Adolph and Louise Luetgert) and Arnold, an adult son from Adolf Luetgert's first marriage.

Police dragged the Chicago River in vain for Louise Luetgert's body. After receiving a tip that the missing woman may have gone "to the country" to visit relatives, Captain Herman Schuettler of the Chicago Police Department extended the range of his search but still could not find her. Schuettler was inclined to believe Mrs. Luetgert was dead. He was also inclined to believe that Luetgert could not be trusted. The list of reasons for his theory grew longer every day.

First of all, Luetgert had not reported his wife missing; her brother had. Diedrich Bicknese had come to Chicago to visit Louise on Tuesday, May 3. Adolph Luetgert informed him that she had been missing since Sunday and told him he had hired private detectives to look for her. Luetgert said he didn't want to go to the police because the publicity would be embarrassing for the family. After looking for his sister for two or three days, Bicknese contacted the authorities, over Luetgert's objections.

On May 16, the *Tribune* revealed that a search of the ashes in the furnace of A. L. Luetgert Sausage & Packing Company at Hermitage and Diversey "brought to light a piece of bone and several pieces of corset steel." Two days later, a headline on the front page announced "Luetgert Held on Wife-Murder Charge." Police had found two gold rings in a vat in the sausage factory. Inside the band of one of the rings were the initials L.L. Mrs. Luetgert always wore her wedding band, which was too large for her, with a smaller ring to keep it from sliding off.

During the trial, which began in August, witnesses testified about quarrels between the Luetgerts, his relationships with other women, Mrs. Luetgert's repeated statements that she was "going away" because she could not bear the shame of her husband's business losses, and the slimy reddish material on the factory floor around the vat in which the gold rings were found.

Spectators crammed the courtroom, which seated about two hundred. Women of all ages, shapes, and sizes stood on tiptoe to get a glimpse of The Sausage King. According to the *Tribune,* Luetgert "looked like a man combed and brushed for his wedding instead of for trial for his life." As the trial progressed, he sat "with his feet on the round of his chair and his thick, fat hands folded . . . looking the least excited and the most unconcerned of all."

State's Attorney Deneen contended that Luetgert had killed his wife and dumped her body in a vat of chemicals at the factory. Luetgert's attorney, William Vincent, described his client as not only innocent but "one of the most infamously wronged men who ever lived in the history of the world." Vincent asserted that Mrs. Luetgert was insane and had wandered away.

As if to prove Vincent's point, sightings of Mrs. Luetgert poured in. She was supposedly spotted in more than a dozen cities in Illinois as well as towns in ten other states. People claimed they saw her on a train, in a saloon, on a barge, and in various mental and physical conditions. Unfortunately for Adolph Luetgert, none of these reports could be substantiated.

The courtroom was oppressively hot throughout the trial, despite open windows and electric fans. As Vincent delivered his closing arguments on Thursday, October 14, he became overwhelmed by the heat and asked for a continuance. Judge Richard Stanley Tuthill allowed him to continue his speech on Saturday.

Vincent finished his closing on Monday with an impassioned plea on behalf of his client: "He has lost his liberty. He has lost his name. He has lost his property. He has lost his wife. Gentlemen of the jury, will you deprive him of his life?"

The gentlemen of the jury mopped their brows and sighed. Like everyone else in Chicago the twelve men—ranging in age from twenty-one to seventy-one—were broiling in the unrelenting heat.

When trial was not in session, they were confined to the third floor of Le Grand Hotel. They could not receive or answer letters. Friends and family were not allowed to visit.

On October 18, the *Tribune* declared: "VERDICT IS IN SIGHT. Luetgert Will Probably Know His Fate in a Few Hours." Anyone who relied on the accuracy of newspaper headlines was doomed to disappointment in this case.

Four days and twenty-two ballots later, the jury staggered back into the courtroom. By then, even Luetgert looked haggard. The jury was hopelessly deadlocked nine to three in favor of conviction.

Luetgert was taken back to jail. Jury selection for the new trial was completed on December 13. The day after that, Luetgert's new attorney, Lawrence Harmon, outlined his defense. The *Tribune* reported, "During Attorney Harmon's speech Luetgert wept frequently, and once his attorney, carried away by his portrayal of the alleged wrongs heaped upon Luetgert, wept also."

Harmon argued that the police had planted the gold rings in the vat at the sausage factory. Luetgert took the stand, breaking down in tears as he talked. Judge Joseph Easton Gary was not impressed, nor was the *Tribune,* which described Luetgert as perfectly egotistical, vain, and stubborn.

Late at night on February 9, after deliberating for about seven hours, the jury pronounced Luetgert guilty of the premeditated murder of his wife, Louise. The Sausage King was sentenced to life imprisonment by Judge Gary on February 19, 1898.

In July of the next year, Adolph Ludwig Luetgert died in his cell at the state penitentiary at Joliet. An autopsy determined that he had probably died of heart disease. Thousands of people attended his funeral. Near the coffin, his children placed a flower arrangement that read: "Our Father's Words, 'I am innocent.'"

Louise Luetgert was never seen again.

THE CAPTAIN'S WAR

1900

Late on the night of May 25, 1900, thirty soldiers marched to the Calumet River, muskets over their shoulders. A supply wagon rumbled behind them. Once aboard the boat that awaited them, General William H. Niles called roll. Only thirteen men answered. The others had deserted, unwilling to risk their lives for the cause.

The boat sailed silently into Lake Michigan following the shoreline. At their destination, the soldiers jumped overboard into the surf and waded ashore, carrying supplies, weapons, and tools.

By the light of a flickering lantern, Niles read a proclamation to the assembled troops. "We will maintain our independence by force of arms to the best of our ability."

The soldiers raised the American flag, dug entrenchments, and erected earthworks, which they roofed over for protection against bombs. Along the outer edge of the territory they intended to hold they placed boards covered with barbed wire. Guards were posted. By 2:00 a.m., everything was in place.

The space the army occupied was a triangle at the foot of Superior Street on Chicago's North Side, with a tract extending about three hundred feet north and south on Lake Shore Drive. Daylight brought the attention of the curious and the scornful, the amused and the hostile. Those who attempted to cross the line were turned away at the point of a bayonet. A police officer in a horse-drawn buggy ignored warnings. His horse was shot, and the bed of the buggy splintered. Niles fired at another officer and missed, wounding a fourteen-year-old boy in the knee.

Soon police patrol wagons carrying more than five hundred police were on their way down Chicago Avenue. Armed with repeating rifles, revolvers, and clubs, the men in blue were prepared to do whatever it took to win the conflict.

Captain George Wellington Streeter was the man most people considered responsible for the battle. Cap Streeter had been a thorn in the side of city government and law enforcement officials since the summer of 1886, when he ran his boat aground on a sandbar about four hundred and fifty feet from the foot of Superior Street. The area under occupation by Niles and his troops was part of Streeter's so-called District of Lake Michigan.

Streeter claimed a storm had smashed his ship into the sandbar; however, weather reports for that night do not mention a storm. The captain got permission from the shoreline owner to leave his boat there temporarily.

Over time, the gap between Streeter's boat and the mainland filled up with sand and debris. By 1893 Streeter claimed ownership of 186 acres, and he was willing to go to war with anyone who tried to tell him he had no legal claim to the area. He even produced a land title (later proven to be a forgery). He denied allegations that he was merely a squatter.

"Shoot," he exclaimed, "when I come here ther warn't a particle of land for me to squat on!"

During the 1890s, Streeter replaced his original boat with a two-story castle made from a high-sided old scow. When real estate men, police officers, or detectives tried to convince him and his wife to leave, they met resistance in the form of sawed-off muskets loaded with birdshot. On one occasion, Streeter's wife poured boiling water from a tea kettle onto three deputies who were attempting to arrest the captain.

The World's Columbian Exposition brought new opportunities for Streeter. Ever the entrepreneur, he refloated his boat and offered sight-seeing excursions. He sold sections of his land to natives and visitors alike.

In 1899, Streeter christened the acreage that surrounded him the District (or Deestric, as he pronounced it) of Lake Michigan and proclaimed himself Territorial Governor. Years later, Everett Ballard quoted Streeter as saying:

> We established our government in the District of Lake Michigan without any flourish of authority or blare of trumpets, and, in fact, without any undue demonstration. One of my outhouses was converted into a temple of justice, and a sign placed above its door proclaimed its august character.

Efforts to oust Streeter through the courts repeatedly failed. He had the District professionally surveyed and platted, paying his own lawyers with deeds of land.

By 1900, Streeter was a familiar figure to Chicagoans—a small, wiry man with shaggy eyebrows, a walrus moustache, and a voice that could be heard above all others as he regaled saloon customers with tall tales peppered with profanity. He was recognizable instantly on the street in his battered stovepipe hat, with his too-large green frock coat hanging loosely from his shoulders.

During the years since Streeter's boat had come ashore, several wealthy families had built magnificent homes on Lake Shore Drive. The view of the lake enhanced their property values; the view of the shacks and shanties in Streeter's "Deestric" did not.

Efforts to evict Streeter escalated, but the captain and his cronies weren't about to give up without a fight. On the night of May 25, 1900, William Niles—the self-styled military governor of the District—brought in his ragtag militia to patrol the boundaries. Armed with clubs, rakes, stones, and guns, they held their own against the initial onslaught by five hundred to six hundred policemen. Streeter insisted that although he and Niles were friends, he had nothing to do with the invasion. The police did not believe him.

As the afternoon of May 26 dragged on and suspense mounted, the number of hobos and squatters protecting the District dwindled. According to newspaper reports the next day, a "sparrow cop" (park policeman) named Hays decided the whole thing had gone far enough. He strolled into the restricted area and confronted the few remaining stalwarts.

"Somebody's liable to get hurt if you keep playing with firearms," he advised them. "And then public sympathy would be dead against you. Surrender to me and you won't get hurt."

They surrendered and were taken into custody. Streeter, despite his protestations that he had nothing to do with the event, was furious.

"It is an outrage on humanity," the newspaper quoted him as saying. "We will teach the officials of the city a lesson, however, and if some of them are not sent to the penitentiary for ten or twelve years you may kick me out of the State of Illinois. They ought to be shot."

No one was sent to the penitentiary, not even Niles and his militia members. Streeter's battle for control of his District of Lake Michigan continued. In March 1902 he was indicted for land fraud. In June he was arrested for the murder of a watchman hired to protect the interests of property-owners on Lake Shore and convicted and sentenced to an "indeterminate" time in prison. He was released after nine months, when new evidence proved that one of his aides had shot the man.

In 1918, Streeter was arrested for selling liquor without a city license and assault on a policeman. On December 10 of that year, agents of the law descended on the District. They moved the captain's possessions into the street, seized his arsenal of guns and ammunition, and tore down his "castle."

On December 11, page 3 of the *Chicago Daily Tribune* featured a photograph titled "Fallen Monarch Watches Ambition's Pyre." There before a bonfire sat Streeter with his dog on his lap. By the captain's side sat his wife, Elma (known as "Ma") and a woman identified as "Mrs. Edwards, a Fellow Squatter."

The next night, Streeter held court in a lean-to constructed from an old wardrobe, several bedsteads, mattresses, carpets, and chairs. A cookstove provided heat. December 16 found him living in a packing box wagon in the middle of the street. The next day, he was ordered to evacuate the District of Lake Michigan within a week. Streeter's glory days had come to an end. He had won many battles but lost the war.

The Streeters ended up on a houseboat on the Calumet River in East Chicago, Indiana. Their boat, called the *Vamoose*, became a floating hot-dog stand serving Municipal Pier and the lakefront. Today, a fashionable neighborhood called Streeterville marks the spot where the captain's "Deestric of Lake Michigan" used to be. Streeterville is home to some of Chicago's tallest skyscrapers as well as upscale stores, hotels, restaurants, and theaters. It incorporates Northwestern University's Feinberg School of Medicine, School of Continuing Studies, and School of Law, as well as the Magnificent Mile portion of Michigan Avenue and Navy Pier.

HIS NEW JOB

1915

It was a busy day at the motion picture studio. In dressing rooms next to the sound stage, actors and actresses donned costumes for their roles in a Russian melodrama. In the personnel office, applicants waited to be interviewed for the less glamorous positions of carpenter, prop man, and stenographer. At a desk on one side of the office sat the receptionist, an officious young man who made it clear to everyone that he was extremely important and terribly busy.

The door opened. In walked a short, slight man with tousled hair, wearing a derby hat that seemed too small for his head. His jacket was too tight and his pants too baggy. Without a sound he seated himself next to a pretty young woman. He smoothed his toothbrush moustache. She smiled coyly. The little man raised his eyebrows and scooted his chair closer to hers.

The door opened again and a small, wiry man in a tan suit entered the office. His moustache was full, like a brush, and his eyes were crossed. He sat down next to the first man and propped one leg on the first man's knee. They began to shove each other.

"Cut!" said a voice. "Let's break for lunch."

In the lunchroom, the two actors who had staged the scuffle mingled with men in Russian military uniforms, women in long skirts and peasant blouses, and other members of the cast and crew. The scene in the personnel office and the Russian melodrama were both part of a comedy film called *His New Job,* the story of a hapless young man who tries to get work at a movie studio and ends up causing a world of trouble.

The year was 1915. The place was Essanay Studios in Chicago. Acting in the film were Ben Turpin (playing the cross-eyed job applicant), Gloria Swanson (playing a stenographer), and Charlotte Mineau (playing a film star). The man in the derby hat and baggy pants was none other than Charles Spencer Chaplin—better known as Charlie Chaplin.

Motion pictures had their beginnings in the late 1800s, with Thomas Edison's Kinetoscope, which was displayed at the World's Columbian Exposition in Chicago in 1893. In the 1900s, Chicago was as big a theater town as New York. An estimated eight thousand to ten thousand theater people lived in Chicago. The city's central location also made it an ideal spot for distribution.

Chaplin had signed with Essanay on January 2, 1915, after working for two years at the Keystone Pictures Studio in California. Keystone's films were fast-paced and violent, with exaggerated movement and gestures. Chaplin's style was more subtle. When Essanay offered him nearly ten times the salary he was receiving from Keystone, along with an opportunity to write and direct his own movies, he headed for Chicago.

Chaplin arrived at Essanay in December 1914. He had been to the Windy City before. A native of Great Britain, he had toured the United States with a vaudeville group in 1910, at age twenty-one. He later wrote in his autobiography: "In 1910, Chicago was attractive in its ugliness, grim and begrimed, a city that still had the spirit of frontier days." He commented that he loved his "grim and seedy" hotel on Wabash Avenue, where "the elevated trains swept by at night and flickered on my bedroom wall like an old-fashioned bioscope."

Unaccustomed to Chicago's bitter cold winters, the actor had not brought a suitable wardrobe. One evening, as he entered a fashionable restaurant he was wearing pajama bottoms around his neck as a scarf.

Actress Gloria Swanson, who would later go on to fame and fortune in Hollywood, was a teenager when Chaplin came to town. She had been cast as an extra in one movie by Essanay but was unsuccessful in getting a larger role in *His New Job*.

"[Charlie Chaplin] reminded me of a pixie from some other world altogether," she wrote in her autobiography, "and for the life of me I couldn't get the feel of his frisky little skits. All morning I felt like a cow trying to dance with a toy poodle."

Reviewing *His New Job* for the *Tribune* on February 2, 1915, Kitty Kelly wrote: "Print yields precedence to picture, for nobody can speak better for himself than Charles Chaplin, even though his speech be of the silent variety. . . The two reels are a genuine rollic of fun which should send warm flutters of financial delight through the Essanay veins."

Unfortunately for Essanay, the "warm flutters of financial delight" provided by Chaplin subsided all too soon. The actor was displeased with Essanay's regimented approach, which he felt limited his creativity, as well as the brusque treatment he had received from Essanay executive George K. Spoor. His dislike for Spoor and for Chicago's weather prompted him to relocate to Essanay in California, and when his contract ended in 1916, he went with the Mutual Film Corporation.

Conditions did not improve for Essanay. Legal problems, the war in Europe, and the departure of several of its stars caused the studio to shut down in 1917. The property on Argyle Street passed through several owners. In March 1996, the Commission on Chicago Landmarks gave monument status to the building that once housed Essanay. Currently it is the home of St. Augustine College. The studio where Chaplin shot *His New Job* is now known as The Charlie Chaplin Auditorium.

A TERRIBLE TIME

1915

The forecast called for showers and thunderstorms, but that didn't deter thousands of people from gathering at the Chicago River the morning of July 24, 1915. For many of them, the Western Electric company picnic was the one great social outing of the year. They looked forward to the cruise across Lake Michigan and the roller coaster rides, parades, races, games, and dancing that awaited them in Michigan City, Indiana. It would take more than the threat of bad weather to keep them away.

Most of the people who congregated on the dock were European immigrants employed by Western Electric's Hawthorne works in Cicero, Illinois. They were thankful to be in America, especially now that the jaws of war held Europe in a death grip. They wondered if the sinking of the British luxury liner *Lusitania* by a German U-boat back on May 7 would persuade the United States to enter the fray. Nearly two thousand civilians had perished on the *Lusitania,* including more than one hundred Americans.

The Polivka sisters—Josephine, Anna, and Mae—were in high spirits when they arrived at the dock near the Clark Street bridge.

Ages nineteen, twenty-two, and twenty-four, they were dressed in white for a parade that would take place later that day.

Their attention was drawn to the steamship *Eastland,* which sat high in the water, waiting to take them to Michigan City. One of five excursion boats chartered for the day, the *Eastland* measured 275 feet overall. She was tall and narrow, with four decks and high-rising steel sides. Originally designed to haul produce across the lake, the ship typically carried fewer than 1,200 passengers. In order to be certified to carry up to 2,570 for the picnic, the owners added three lifeboats and six life rafts to those that already hung from the stanchions along the *Eastland's* hurricane deck.

Carrying extra lifeboats and rafts for an increased number of passengers seemed logical and prudent to a lot of people. A. A. Schantz, general manager of the Detroit & Cleveland Navigation Company, thought otherwise. Schantz warned that mounting extra lifeboats and rafts would make lake boats top-heavy and unseaworthy. He believed that the additional weight on the upper decks would cause some of the boats to "turn turtle."

At 6:40 a.m. on July 24, 1915, the crew of the *Eastland* began loading passengers. Charles Agnastoklio, a Western Electric mechanic, was one of the first to board. He noticed that the boat seemed top-heavy. At 6:41 a.m. the ship began to list to starboard. The crew corrected the tilt. Three minutes later, the ship listed slightly to port. It was righted. At 7:00, the *Eastland* listed to port again. By then, there were a thousand passengers aboard.

In a letter to his mother, passenger Bert Cross later wrote: "When the boat started to list toward the river, I was not alarmed. I knew the boat to be cranky."

What Cross did not know was that the hardwood flooring in the forward dining room on the cabin level had recently been replaced with two inches of concrete. In addition, a layer of cement had been laid near the aft gangway. This added fifteen to twenty tons of weight. The extra weight coupled with the extra lifeboats and life rafts made the ship not only "cranky" but top-heavy to a dangerous degree.

At 7:10 a.m. the *Eastland* reached its capacity of 2,500 passengers and 70 crew. On the promenade deck aft, Bradfield's Orchestra began to play ragtime music. People started dancing. The gangplank was drawn in at 7:18.

By then, the list to port was twenty to twenty-five degrees. No attempt was made to get people off the boat. Onboard, the passengers were still enjoying themselves, in spite of the tilting floors.

It was 7:28 a.m. Standing near the rail toward the front of the boat, passenger James Peterson heard a noise that sounded to him like beer cases falling over. "I dropped my cane," he wrote later, "and it went slipping across the deck toward the cabin. I leaned over to reach for it but before I could grab it I was kicking about in the water."

When the *Eastland* rolled over, people seated in chairs on deck were hurled into the Chicago River. There was no time to hand out life jackets or launch lifeboats. Water rushed in, flooding staterooms and cabins. Panicked passengers jammed the staircases.

"There were screams and we were thrown to the side," Josephine Polivka said years later. "People were grabbing at us from below. I remember hands reaching out from the water."

On shore, journalist Harlan E. Babcock gasped in horror as the vessel careened on its side. "In an instant," he wrote, "the surface of the river was black with struggling, crying, frightened, drowning humanity."

Rescue efforts began even before the *Eastland* settled in the mud. Despite the quick response, it was too late for more than eight hundred of the *Eastland's* passengers. The ship lay in twenty feet of water with her bow just over nineteen feet from the wharf, but many victims could not swim. Falling wreckage trapped hundreds.

Wet woolen suits and layered garments acted like weights, dragging people down.

"I drank that Chicago river water," Charles Agnastoklio said, "and—*oohhh*—it was bad."

By Saturday afternoon, a central morgue had been established in the Second Regiment Armory on Washington Boulevard at Curtis Street. The bodies of victims were laid in rows and assigned numbers. Shortly after midnight, people were allowed to enter and make identification. A report prepared by the American Red Cross stated: "The heartrending scenes of the Armory had better be left undescribed."

Most of the victims had lived in Berwyn and Cicero or on the far West Side of Chicago, not far from the Hawthorne plant. On July 28 alone, thirty to forty funerals were scheduled.

Peterson and Agnastoklio survived, as did the Polivka sisters. "It was a terrible time," Josephine Polivka said. "There was a wreath on nearly every door."

"The ugliest of the facts," declared the *Chicago Tribune* on July 27, perhaps referring to Schantz's warning, "is that . . . what was expected and predicted happened."

A crew of thirty-two men worked sixteen days, twelve to fourteen hours per day, to right the *Eastland*. The ship was turned over to its owners, the St. Joseph-Chicago Steamship Company, on August 14. Criminal and civil suits were filed on behalf of the victims at state and federal levels. In February 1916, Judge Clarence Sessions found the defendants not guilty of conspiracy to defraud the government. Civil litigation continued for twenty years. Two key defendants in the civil actions passed away before guilt or innocence could be determined. Joseph Erickson, the *Eastland*'s chief engineer, was convicted posthumously.

The Hawthorne Works never had another picnic cruise.

"SAY IT AIN'T SO!"

1919

In the weeks leading up to the 1919 World Series, headlines in the *New York Times* made it clear that both the Chicago White Sox and the Cincinnati Reds were capable of winning the trophy. Then, on September 27, with the first game of the Series just four days away, the *New York Times* announced: "Betting on World's Series Result Now Finds White Sox Favored at 7 to 10."

Pitcher Eddie Cicotte was one reason the Sox were favored. Acquired from the Boston Red Sox in 1912, Cicotte had won twenty-nine games for Chicago in the 1919 regular season. In October, when the odds shifted to 5 to 6 in favor of the Sox, the *New York Times* explained the change:

> *It was apparent that National League fans have been afraid only of the sterling right arm of Cicotte. With the report that he was nursing a sore arm, they began "kicking in" with an enthusiasm that made all hands sit up and take a quantity of notice.*

There was more "kicking in" to come. On October 2, after the Reds slammed the White Sox 9 to 1, the Reds were suddenly listed by the *New York Times* as 7 to 10 betting favorites.

"With Cicotte out of the way," the newspaper said, "the followers of the Cincinnati Reds feel confident that the National League pennant winners will skip through the series to a quick and decisive victory."

The Reds won again on October 2. The White Sox won game three, but the Reds stormed back to take games four and five. A headline in the *Chicago Daily Tribune* on October 7 blared: "What Is Wrong with White Sox? Gleason Asks." White Sox manager Kid Gleason was quoted as saying: "The bunch I had fighting in August for the pennant would have trimmed this Cincinnati bunch without a struggle. The bunch I have now couldn't beat a high school team."

Among those who had a possible answer to the question posed by the headline was Hugh Fullerton, reporter for the *Chicago Herald and Examiner.* Even before the first game, Fullerton had heard rumors that the Series was "fixed" in favor of the Reds. The sudden, major shift in betting seemed to support those rumors. Fullerton decided to circle suspicious plays on his scorecard as he watched the Series. He sent a wire to newspapers: "Advise all not to bet on this Series. Ugly rumors afloat."

Fuller wasn't the only one with suspicions. The morning after the first game, White Sox owner Charlie Comiskey called John A. Heydler, president of the National League.

"Something is wrong with the team," Comiskey told Heydler.

Heydler responded that perhaps the White Sox had underestimated Cincinnati's strength.

After the second game, Comiskey contacted Heydler again. He told Heydler about a Chicago fan who had wagered on Cincinnati after getting some "inside information." According to Comiskey, manager Kid Gleason was also suspicious about the behavior of some of his players.

The Sox beat the Reds in game six at Redland Field. However, Chicago dropped game seven, also at Redland. The Reds now led the Sox four games to three.

Game eight was played on October 9. In the first inning, White Sox pitcher Claude Williams gave up four straight one-out hits, yielding three runs for the Reds. Relief pitcher Big Bill James allowed one of Williams's base runners to score. James's performance throughout the rest of the game was lackluster at best. "Shoeless" Joe Jackson scored a home run for Chicago in the third inning, and a Chicago rally in the eighth added four more runs to the scoreboard—but by then the Reds had scored ten runs. Jackson grounded out in the ninth to end the World Series.

The *Chicago Daily Tribune* did not mince words: "Sox Handed Real Mauling in Final, 10-5 . . . Now We Know How Casey Felt After He Fanned."

"The White Sox folded up like an umbrella," observed the *New York Times*.

Reporter Fullerton, who had identified quite a few questionable plays, issued an ominous and cryptic statement in his column on October 10: "There are seven men on the team who will not be there when the gong sounds next Spring and some of them will not be in either major league."

Over the next few months, many attempts were made to explain the outcome of the Series. Some said the White Sox were careless or out of condition or that their star pitchers were tired. On November 2, American League umpire Billy Evans expressed his views: "The Chicago club did not play anywhere near up to its standard."

Rumors continued to fly. Comiskey undertook an investigation. On December 15, he announced: "I am now very happy to state that we have discovered nothing to indicate any member of my team double-crossed me or the public last fall."

August Herrmann, president of the Cincinnati Reds and head of the National Baseball Commission, refused to make any comment about the World Series beyond saying that all the stories had been investigated and declared without foundation.

Fullerton was not convinced. He wrote articles calling for "straight talk" on the subject of gambling in baseball in general and the 1919 World Series in particular. He declared that major league baseball was in crisis. He was ridiculed in popular baseball magazines, where he was accused of being ignorant about the sport and of spreading wild, ugly rumors obtained from bar-room conversations.

It took a rumor concerning another baseball game to bring everything to a head.

On August 31, 1920, William L. Veeck, president of the Chicago Cubs, received a telegram advising him of rumors that a routine game between the Cubs and the Philadelphia Phillies was fixed. Similar telegrams and phone calls followed. Veeck had them traced, hoping that he could get to the bottom of the matter without anyone in the media finding out. Not only was he unable to determine the identity of those who had warned him, but on September 4, the Chicago *Herald and Examiner* broadcast the story far and wide.

Prominent Chicago businessman and baseball fan Fred M. Loomis spoke for thousands in a letter to the *Chicago Daily Tribune:*

> *Where there is so much smoke there must be some fire. . .*
> *The game must be cleaned up and it must be cleaned*
> *up at once. Those who have in their possession the*

evidence of gambling last fall in the world series should come forward with it.

On September 7, at the request of Chief Justice Charles Mac-Donald of Cook County's Criminal Courts Division, a grand jury was convened. MacDonald announced that the investigation into gambling in baseball would include the 1919 World Series. A little over two weeks later, the *Chicago Daily Tribune* quoted Assistant State's Attorney Hartley Replogle: "The last world series between the Chicago White Sox and the Cincinnati Reds was not on the square. From five to seven players on the White Sox team are involved."

Eddie Cicotte and Joe Jackson testified before the grand jury on September 28. Cicotte confessed that he had been bribed ten thousand dollars to throw the 1919 World Series. Jackson had been promised twenty thousand but had only received five thousand. Cicotte and Jackson implicated players Charles (Swede) Risberg, George (Buck) Weaver, Arnold (Chick) Gandil, Fred McMullin, and Oscar (Happy) Felsch in the plot. As Cicotte and Jackson left the courtroom, a throng of photographers and reporters surrounded them. According to a newspaper story by sportswriter Charley Owens, a boy tagged along after Jackson, clutching at his sleeve, pleading, "Say it ain't so, Joe."

On October 22, the grand jury ended its hearings on the matter. Indictments were handed down for eight Chicago players along with a significant number of gamblers who had been involved. Almost ten months later, in August 1921, a jury acquitted the "Black Sox" (as the accused players had come to be known) of the charge of conspiring to throw the 1919 World Series games.

Even though they were acquitted, the Black Sox were banned from major and minor league baseball. They all played semipro and outlaw baseball for a time, then pursued other occupations.

In the years that followed the scandal, the story of the boy who tugged on "Shoeless" Joe's sleeve became a legend. Jackson himself debunked the tale, insisting that Charley Owens made it up.

John Christgau offered another version of the story in 2005. His article in the baseball magazine *Nine* told of Roland (Roly) Gehre, who was ten years old and lived in a Chicago suburb at the time of the Black Sox scandal. In interviews with members of Gehre's family, Christgau learned that up until Gehre died in 1989, he persisted in telling the story of how he accompanied his uncle to the courthouse in September 1920. When Roly saw his hero emerge from the courtroom, he couldn't help shouting, "Just say it ain't so, Joe. Say it ain't so!" Jackson did not acknowledge him.

TRUTH, JUSTICE, AND
THE *DAILY NEWS*

1924

On May 21, 1924, thirteen-year-old Bobby Franks of Chicago went missing.

Jacob and Flora Franks became concerned when their son failed to arrive home for dinner. By late that evening, they were frantic. Jacob Franks asked a longtime friend, attorney Samuel Ettelson, to help him search for the boy.

While the two men were out, the telephone rang at the Franks residence. Bobby's mother answered. A man identifying himself as George Johnson told her that her son had been kidnapped but that he was safe, and that she should wait for further instructions. Mrs. Franks fainted.

Over at the *Chicago Daily News,* reporter James W. Mulroy was contacted by an anonymous caller who told him:

"There's been a kidnapping. Sam Ettelson knows all about it."

Mulroy knew that the message might be a hoax, but he didn't mind checking it out. Jacob Franks was extremely wealthy. It was not hard to believe that someone might kidnap a member of his family and demand a ransom. He tracked down Ettelson at the Franks home, an impressive three-story dwelling on Ellis Avenue. Although Ettelson finally admitted to Mulroy that Bobby Franks had been kidnapped, the newspaper refrained from printing the story to avoid endangering Bobby's life.

The next morning, another *Daily News* reporter, Alvin H. Goldstein, was sent to investigate a possible homicide. The body of a young boy had been found in a culvert about twenty miles south of Chicago. A pair of horn-rimmed spectacles was found near the body.

Franks refused to believe that the victim could be his son. Bobby did not wear glasses. Besides, Franks had received a ransom note from the kidnappers that morning, demanding ten thousand dollars.

"Should you carefully follow out our instructions to the letter," the note said, "we can assure you that your son will be safely returned to you within six hours of our receipt of the money." The note was signed "Yours truly, George Johnson."

Shortly after 3:00 that afternoon, "George Johnson" called the Franks home. He said that he was sending a cab to pick Franks up, and that Franks was to go to a drugstore at 1465 East Sixty-Third Street. Franks and Ettelson both listened to the instructions but when the cab arrived, neither one could remember the specific address given by the kidnapper. The cab driver knew only where to pick Franks up, not where to take him.

As Franks and Ettelson struggled to recall more than just the name of the street, the telephone rang again. It was Franks' brother-in-law, who had been persuaded to visit the morgue to identify the body found earlier that day.

"Jake, I'm sorry," he said, "I'm so sorry. The boy they found in the culvert near Hammond . . . It's Bobby."

The kidnapping was now a murder. Mulroy and Goldstein were determined to break the case wide open.

During one of their visits to the Franks home, the pair encountered a neighbor and distant relative of Franks: eighteen-year-old University of Chicago student Richard Loeb. An avid reader of detective stories, Loeb was eager to help in the investigation. He suggested that the reporters start by trying to determine which drugstore on Sixty-Third Street the kidnapper had specified. All they had to do, Loeb put forth, was canvas the stores to see if anyone had called asking for Jacob Franks. He even offered to chauffeur the two *Daily News* reporters, along with Howard Mayer, the University of Chicago's campus correspondent for the *Evening American*. Mayer had known Loeb for about a year.

Their search bore fruit at Van de Bogert & Ross. A druggist remembered getting more than one telephone call for Mr. Franks on May 22. Loeb seemed delighted that his idea had paid off.

"This is what comes from reading detective stories!" he boasted.

Loeb made several other comments, one of which struck the reporters as peculiar, even disturbing.

"If I were going to murder anybody," he said. "I would murder just such a cocky little SOB as Bobby Franks."

While Loeb and the reporters tracked down drugstores, police continued to investigate the eyeglasses left at the murder scene. The *Tribune* ran a picture of the glasses under the heading: "Whose Spectacles Are These?" A detailed description followed. Investigators caught a break when an optician told them the hinges were unusual. It turned out that only three eyeglasses with that type of hinge had been sold in the Chicago area. Two of the people who had purchased them were ruled out as suspects. The third, nineteen-year-old Nathan Leopold Jr., admitted they were his. Leopold explained that he had often been to the area where the body was found in his search for unusual types of birds. He told detectives that his glasses must have fallen out of his pocket on one of his birding trips.

The police were skeptical. They became even more skeptical when they discovered that Leopold was a close friend of Richard Loeb, who had been so helpful to reporters and detectives covering the Franks case. In fact, Leopold acknowledged that on May 21 he and Loeb had spent much of the day together. Loeb was brought in for questioning.

In the meantime, Goldstein and Mulroy wondered if they might be able to find a sample of something typed by either of the two suspects. If so, they could compare it with the ransom note sent to Jacob Franks. A visit to the University of Chicago campus turned up carbon copies of study sheets Loeb had typed and shared with other students. Experts determined that several of the study sheets and the ransom note had been typed on the same machine, which had a defective letter T.

Although the reporters could not find the typewriter at Leopold's residence, a maid said she had seen a portable typewriter recently in the home. The evidence was beginning to add up and it wasn't long before Leopold and Loeb confessed to the kidnapping and murder of Bobby Franks. The two boys—both from wealthy families, both highly intelligent—said they simply wanted to see if they could commit the perfect crime.

On a sweltering day in August 1924, attorney Clarence Darrow cleared his throat and began a speech that he hoped would convince Judge John Caverly to sentence Leopold and Loeb to life in prison rather than death by hanging. State's Attorney Robert Crowe maintained that hanging was the most appropriate punishment for the defendants, whom he described as snakes, mad dogs, and spoiled smart alecks.

Darrow's impassioned plea against applying the death penalty worked. Based on consideration for their age and the possible benefits to criminology that might come from studying them, Judge Caverly sentenced Leopold and Loeb to life in prison for the murder, plus ninety-nine years for the kidnapping for ransom of Robert Franks.

In 1925 James Mulroy and Alvin Goldstein won the Pulitzer Prize for Reporting "for their service toward the solution of the murder of Robert Franks . . . and the bringing to justice of Nathan F. Leopold and Richard Loeb."

"WE MUST HAVE TICKETS!"

1925

"The whole town rose up on its hind legs and shouted, 'We must have tickets!'" wrote Irving Vaughan in the *Chicago Daily Tribune*, November 24, 1925.

The town's determination to get tickets to the game between the Chicago Bears and the Chicago Cardinals created what the *Tribune* described as "a miniature riot." Prospective customers stormed the ticket office as soon as tickets went on sale. South State Street "became a bedlam." Mounted and foot police finally restored a semblance of order by swinging customers into a single line that "extended from the ticket booth in the back of the store out to the sidewalk, down to the corner of Adams Street, then east to the alley, into the alley a hundred feet or more and out to the sidewalk again."

Similar events in Chicago usually drew anywhere from 1,000 to 14,000 spectators. This time, all 28,000 reserve seats were sold before nightfall. The next day, bleacher seats and standing room tickets went on sale. Again, customers besieged the ticket office and created traffic jams. The *Tribune* reported that around 7,000 tickets were sold before the manager closed down the ticket booth, amidst wailing and gnashing of teeth.

On a cloudy, chilly Thanksgiving Day in 1925, thousands of lucky ticket holders crammed themselves into Cubs Park (now Wrigley Field). The day after the event, the newspaper estimated that "paid attendance ran over the 40,000 mark." Years later, the number 39,000 would be offered up as the final tally.

This particular game between the Chicago Bears and the Chicago Cardinals was nothing special in and of itself. There was certainly nothing new or impressive about the uniforms: dog-ear, brown leather helmets (some with the flaps down, others with the flaps up), wool jerseys with strips of material sewn on the front, brown canvas pants, woolen socks, and cleated shoes.

What the fans yearned for, what they paid for, and what they came for that day was to see one player, the newest member of the Chicago Bears, a young man nimbly described by sportswriter Grantland Rice as:

> *A streak of fire, a breath of flame*
> *Eluding all who reach and clutch;*
> *A gray ghost thrown into the game*
> *That rival hands may never touch;*
> *A rubber bounding, blasting soul*
> *Whose destination is the goal—Red Grange of Illinois!*

Twenty-two-year-old Harold E. Grange—Number Seventy-Seven—was known by football fans everywhere as one of the greatest halfbacks ever to play for the University of Illinois. He was called "Red" because of his auburn hair. His running style earned him the nickname "The Galloping Ghost." Sportswriter Paul Gallico described Grange's style as "a peculiar sliding motion and wonderfully timed weaving of the hips that always kept his body moving away from the point of impact."

Grange, who stood five foot eleven inches and weighed 175 pounds, had a simple explanation: "If you have the football and eleven guys are after you, if you're smart, you'll run."

In 1924, Grange had delivered what is considered by some to be the greatest single-game performance in the history of college football. He scored four times in the first twelve minutes, scored again in the third quarter, and wrapped up his day by completing a touchdown pass for the Fighting Illini's final score in a 39-14 rout of the Michigan Wolverines.

In 1925, many professional football teams were struggling financially; some were on the verge of collapse. College football was the big sport at the time, and its players were held in high esteem. In contrast, many people viewed professional football as undignified, even sleazy. Some suspected that only those who couldn't find respectable work would play pro football. Sportswriter John Underwood described pro football as "a dirty little business run by rogues and bargain-basement entrepreneurs."

Grange was reported to have said, "I'd have been more popular with the colleges if I had joined Capone's mob in Chicago rather than the Bears."

A letter to the editor printed in the *New York Times* in 1925 asserted:

> *The gridiron stars of the past have fought their battles*
> *and won their niche in the collegiate halls of fame,*
> *and when the great four years were over they hung up*
> *those muddy moleskins in the fieldhouse and joined the*
> *ranks of truly professional men . . . to serve humanity*

*in some measure. Thus the old game has been preserved
as a distinctly college affair. Tradition associates it with
those four years of youth—where it belongs.*

An editorial published that same year in the *Chicago Tribune*
expressed an opposing view:

> *Grange might go into the bond business, real estate or
> insurance. Doors would open when his card came. . . .
> But if Grange proposes to make money by doing some-
> thing he knows how to do and something that people
> have been paying, and praying, to see him do, then he
> knocks off a lot of collegiate moss. We don't get it.*

On Thanksgiving Day, as former Northwestern University
standout John Leo "Paddy" Driscoll prepared to punt for the Cardinals, he was not thinking about the pros and cons of professional
sports or about what people were paying, and praying, to see. His
primary thought was to keep the ball out of the hands of Number
Seventy-Seven, the Galloping Ghost.

The fans booed loudly every time Driscoll angled a kick away
from Grange. After the game, Driscoll reportedly commented to
his wife that it was terrible the way the fans booed Grange. His wife
explained: "They weren't booing Red. They were booing you for
not kicking to him." "Gosh," responded Paddy, "kicking a football
to Red Grange would be like grooving a baseball to Babe Ruth. It's
something to be avoided whenever possible."

Grange gained a total of 92 yards that day. The game, described
by Irving Vaughan as "hard driving but thrilling," ended in a zero
to zero tie. Three days later, the Bears played the Columbus Tigers

at Cubs Park. A heavy snowstorm failed to discourage about 28,000 fans from watching the Bears squeak by the Tigers. The red-haired apparition played a much better game, despite an icy field.

The two Chicago games were just the beginning of two barnstorming tours planned by Bears coach George Halas, who hoped to not only capitalize on his acquisition of Grange but to kindle national support for pro football. Between November 26 and January 31, the Galloping Ghost and his teammates traveled coast to coast and played a grueling schedule of seventeen exhibition games. In New York, a crowd of 65,000 turned out to see the Bears beat the Giants. In Los Angeles, spectators of a Bears-Tigers game numbered 75,000. Pro football was on its way to victory, and it never looked back.

After retiring from football, Grange worked in the insurance business and later became a sports broadcaster. He was a charter member of both the College Football Hall of Fame and Pro Football Hall of Fame. He died in 1991 at age eighty-seven.

As a member of the Chicago Bears, he gave the game of professional football the legitimacy it needed to become a success. Surveys indicate that pro football is more popular today than any other sport among American males age twelve and older.

And to think that the ball really got rolling in Chicago one November day in 1925, when "the whole town rose up on its hind legs and shouted, 'We must have tickets!'"

It was the largest crowd that had ever gathered to watch professional football.

"MY SON WAS NOT A GANGSTER"

1929

Reinhart Schwimmer slipped into an overcoat, buttoned it, and draped a wool scarf around his neck. The temperature outside was well below freezing, and the harsh winter wind was certain to make it feel even colder. He ran his fingers along the brim of his stylish felt hat.

It was February 14, Valentine's Day, and Schwimmer was meeting his mother for lunch. He also planned to stop by the SMC Cartage Company for a cup of coffee with some of his friends. His mother didn't approve of his friends.

"They're hoodlums . . . gangsters . . . criminals!" she always exclaimed with a shudder. "They'll be the death of you. I know these things. I always know these things."

A gust of icy wind stung the optician's face as he opened the front door of the Parkway Hotel, where he lived. As he stood in the snow waiting for a streetcar, he tried not to think about his mother's warnings. It was true that his friends were involved in gambling, prostitution, and "bootlegging"—the illegal production and distribution of liquor. They were members of the North Side Gang, headed by George "Bugs" Moran. Practically everything they did was illegal.

Not only that, violence between rival gangs had picked up steam about ten years earlier. Big Jim Colosimo had been shot to death in the lobby of the South Wabash Café. Gang leader Dean O'Banion had been murdered in his flower shop. Whether you worked for Moran or "Scarface" Al Capone or some other big cheese, you had to watch your back.

Schwimmer knew his mother couldn't possibly understand how much fun he had playing the ponies and dining at swanky hotels. He loved the look of respect in people's eyes when they realized what a hard-boiled guy he must be. Moran's boys called him "Dr. Schwimmer" and counted on him for advice when they wanted to dress or behave in a high-class, gentlemanly manner.

It was snowing lightly at 10:25 a.m. when Schwimmer arrived at SMC Cartage Company, a one-story red brick structure on Clark Street. Several trucks stood against side walls in the unheated garage. Another truck was jacked up in the center of the concrete floor. Mechanic John May's dog, Highball, was tied by his leash to the axle. Five men in coats and hats were gathered around a coffeepot. Schwimmer could see the men's faces clearly in the glaring light of the 200-watt bulb that burned overhead. They were Pete and Frank Gusenberg, Al Kachellek, Adam Heyer, and Al Weinshank. John May scooted out from under the truck that was up on jacks. He wiped his hands on his oil-smeared overalls and walked toward the group.

The optician hadn't expected to see so many of Moran's men in the garage that morning. He noticed that everyone except May was dressed in formal attire, like they were going to a big meeting. Schwimmer wondered if Moran himself would show up.

"Hello, boys," someone said.

Schwimmer turned and saw two policemen. He realized they must have entered the building not long after he did. The Gusenbergs drew their guns but then relaxed.

"Coppers," one of them muttered. "Just what we need."

The gang seemed more annoyed than anything else. Cops conducted shakedowns from time to time, mostly for show. All you had to do was pay them off.

"Put your guns on the table," ordered one of the policemen.

The men did as they were told.

"Now, hands on the wall."

Kachellek and the others rolled their eyes in irritation but turned toward the whitewashed wall and placed their palms against it. The first spray of bullets caught Schwimmer completely by surprise. Waves of pain and panic surged through him. *What kind of gun makes a sound like that?* he wondered. *A Tommy gun? Do cops carry Tommy guns? Oh, my god, I'm going to die.*

He was right. Ten minutes later, he and the Gusenbergs, Kachellek, Heyer, Weinshank, and May lay sprawled on the floor, blood flowing from multiple wounds delivered by Thompson submachine guns, sawed-off shotguns, and a .45 caliber pistol.

Before long, the place was swarming with real police officers. It was later determined that the two "policemen" who had surprised Moran's men were imposters. Once Moran's men were disarmed, two men armed with submachine guns stepped around the corner and opened fire. Witnesses who saw the four men leaving the garage assumed police were taking two criminals into custody and that everything was under control.

Reporter Walter Trohan described what he saw when he arrived at the building on Clark Street that Valentine's Day in 1929: "There were just pools of blood everywhere and the dead guys spread out all over as in the movies. I'd never seen that many before. They were sprawled all over . . . and this wild German shepherd was barking and crazy and lunging on a heavy chain."

The headline in the *Chicago Daily Tribune* on February 15 screamed, "SLAY DOCTOR IN MASSACRE." The article noted that Dr. Schwimmer "had no criminal record, but was known as the companion of hoodlums and was said to have boasted recently that he was in the alky racket and could have any one 'taken for a ride.'" ("Taking someone for a ride" meant shoving them into a car and killing them during the drive.)

Schwimmer's sixty-year-old mother, Josephine, was so distraught she had to ask a friend to identify her son's body. "No, no, no, my son was not a gangster," the newspaper quoted her as saying. "He was always a good boy, until he got to going around with that North Side gang. I told him months ago that his doom was coming. I warned him, but he had no faith in me."

It is generally accepted that Bugs Moran was the target in the St. Valentine's Day massacre. Lookouts apparently misidentified one of the other men as Moran, and gave the signal for the killers to proceed. It seems likely that the shooters were out-of-town "guns for hire" and had never met the gang leader. They murdered everyone in the garage, assuming one of them must be Moran.

From early on, Al Capone was a chief suspect. He was in Miami at the time and claimed he was not involved. But no one believed him. The massacre catapulted him to infamy as a master criminal of superhuman proportions—an outlaw for the ages.

Following the massacre, President Herbert Hoover declared, "I want [Capone] in jail." Hoover got his wish in October 1931, when "Big Al" was convicted of income tax evasion. In 1939, suffering from syphilis, Capone was released. He lived as an invalid and recluse in Florida until his death in 1947, at age forty-eight. George "Bugs" Moran died of lung cancer in prison in 1957, while serving time for bank robbery.

Reinhart Schwimmer was buried in Chicago's Rosehill Cemetery. The building on Clark Street where the massacre occurred was torn down in 1967. No one was ever charged with the murders that took place there on Valentine's Day, 1929.

JOURNEY TO A NEW WORLD

1942

The guests began to arrive shortly after 8:00 on the evening of December 2, 1942. To their hostess Laura's surprise, every man who walked through the front door that night made a point of congratulating her husband. He accepted their praise with a modest grin but said nothing in response.

Laura queried her guests: "Tell me what Enrico did to earn these congratulations."

"Don't get excited," one person replied. "You'll find out sometime."

"Nothing special," another said. "He's a smart guy. That's all."

As the party continued, guests gathered in the living room to discuss the war. For the past three years, Britain, France, Australia, and New Zealand had been fighting Germany and its supporters, Italy and Japan. On December 7, 1941, Japanese planes had bombed Pearl Harbor in Hawaii, and the United States had entered the conflict.

Long before that, conditions in Europe had impelled Laura Capón Fermi and her husband, Enrico, to leave their homeland.

Natives of Italy, they and their two children traveled to Sweden in 1938 so that Fermi could accept the Nobel Prize in Physics. The Italian Fascist press criticized him for not wearing a Fascist uniform and for failing to give the Fascist salute when he received the award. Of even greater concern to Fermi was the fact that Italy's new racial laws discriminated against Jews and deprived them of most of their civil rights. Laura was Jewish. The Fermis decided not to return to Italy. After the ceremony in Sweden, they proceeded to London and from there to America.

Not long after the Fermis fled Italy, German scientists discovered fission, or the splitting of the uranium atom, opening the door to the creation of nuclear (atomic) energy. Fermi—who had achieved nuclear fission about four years earlier—was concerned that any further findings might help the Nazis. He and several of his colleagues in the United States agreed to delay publication of any breakthroughs they might achieve.

Noted physicist Albert Einstein sent an urgent letter to President Franklin D. Roosevelt, warning that atomic energy could be used in the construction of bombs. The thought of an atom bomb in the possession of Hitler's Germany spurred the United States to intensify its own efforts to create and harness the chain reaction Einstein described.

In February 1940, funds were made available to start research. Eventually the endeavor became known by the code name "Manhattan Project" because much of the early research was performed at Columbia University in Manhattan.

Enrico Fermi was chosen to lead a team of scientists in producing a controlled, self-sustaining nuclear chain reaction. When the project was moved to the University of Chicago, it was discovered that suitable locations for a laboratory had all been requisitioned by armed forces stationed in the area.

Arthur H. Compton, a physics professor, located a squash court under the stands of the school's football stadium. The space— approximately thirty feet wide by sixty feet long and twenty-six feet high—was available because the University of Chicago's president, Robert M. Hutchins, had banned varsity football from the campus.

Recalling the process, Fermi wrote: "An outsider . . . would have seen only what appeared to be a crude pile of black bricks and wooden timbers. All but one side of the pile was obscured by a balloon cloth envelope."

First, the scientists conducted tests on thirty piles constructed of uranium embedded in a matrix of graphite. (These test piles were smaller than the size necessary to establish a chain reaction.) When construction of a full-sized pile began, two crews worked almost around the clock in the November cold. For security reasons, the scientists refused to ask for heat.

Laura Fermi knew only that her husband went to work every day at the Metallurgical Laboratory or "Met. Lab." In her book *Atoms in the Family,* she wrote: "Everything was top secret there. I was told one single secret: There were no metallurgists at the Metallurgical Laboratory. Even this piece of information was not to be divulged."

Recalling the project, Fermi wrote: "Finally, the day came when we were ready to run the experiment. We gathered on a balcony about 10 feet above the floor of the large room in which the structure had been erected."

About fifty scientists and spectators were in attendance. Fermi's plan called for three sets of neutron-absorbing control rods to be gradually removed from the pile, one after the other. A control rod would act as starter, accelerator, and brake for the reaction. Every possible precaution was taken against an accident.

At 9:45 a.m. on December 2, 1942, Fermi ordered the first set of rods removed from the pile. Counters clicked. A quivering pen recorded the neutron activity within the pile. At each step of the way, the operation of the pile conformed closely with Fermi's calculations. A young scientist named George Weil started to withdraw the main control rod. The counters clicked faster and faster. Suddenly the automatic control rods slammed home with a loud clang. They had been set for too low a neutron count, causing the operation to shut down prematurely.

It was 11:35.

"Let's go to lunch," Fermi said.

The team was back in place at the pile by 2:00.

Fermi described what happened next: "At 2:30, Weil pulled out the control rod in a series of measured adjustments. Shortly after, the intensity shown by the indicators began to rise at a slow but ever-increasing rate. At this moment we knew that the self-sustaining reaction was under way."

The group watched, spellbound, for twenty-eight minutes while the world's first nuclear chain reactor operated.

"The event was not spectacular," Fermi wrote later, "no fuses burned, no lights flashed. But to us it meant that release of atomic energy on a large scale would be only a matter of time."

After the reaction was stopped, Eugene Wigner presented Fermi with a bottle of Chianti wine. Arthur Compton telephoned James B. Conant at Harvard. Referencing Columbus's arrival in America in 1492, Compton said: "The Italian navigator has landed in the New World."

"How were the natives?" asked Conant.

"Very friendly," was the response.

Further development of atomic energy over the next three years focused on producing an effective weapon. In May 1945, Germany surrendered to the Allies. In August, atomic bombs were dropped on Hiroshima and Nagasaki, ending the war with Japan. World War II was over.

Not long after the end of the war, Fermi handed a paperbound volume to his wife, Laura. It contained information on atomic energy, recently declassified and released for publication. Laura worked her way through the book, struggling with its technical language. Somewhere near the middle, she found the reason for the congratulations her husband had received at the party back in December 1942.

Enrico and Laura Fermi never returned to Italy. Enrico died in Chicago in 1954 at age fifty-three. His wife died in 1977. Unlike her husband, she lived to see the world's first commercial nuclear power station, opened in England in 1956, and the first commercial nuclear generator to become operational in the United States a year later. Both facilities owed their existence to the atomic pile built by Fermi and his colleagues under the stands at a football stadium in Chicago.

THE $5,000 REWARD

1944

On December 9, 1932, patrolman William D. Lundy was drinking a cup of hot coffee at Vera Walush's delicatessen on South Ashland Avenue, trying to warm up after walking his beat in bone-chilling five-degree weather. The next minute, two robbers burst through the deli's door. At age fifty-five, Lundy was on the heavy side but still a strong man. He lunged at one of the bandits. Within minutes, the police officer lay dead on the floor, shot six times in the back by the second robber. The bullet penetrated his heart, guaranteeing that he would not live to see his wife and three children again. The thieves grabbed the money from the cash register and bolted out of the deli, escaping in an automobile with an Ohio license plate.

On December 11, the *Chicago Daily Tribune* announced that police had arrested ten suspects in the murder and were holding them for possible identification by Vera Walush. They were also seeking a man named Ted Marcinkiewicz who had supposedly threatened to rob the delicatessen. One month later, Marcinkiewicz and a man named Joseph Majczek found themselves on trial for murder.

The defendants both had alibis, but Vera Walush identified them as the robbers. After deliberating for nearly three hours, the jury returned a verdict of guilty. Marcinkiewicz and Majczek were sentenced to ninety-nine years each in the penitentiary.

"The two men took the verdict with no outward expression," the *Daily Tribune* reported, "but their wives, who had been in court since the trial started, screamed at the announcement of their fate."

Lundy's widow and children were said to be "content." Also content was Mayor Anton Cermak, whose promise to clean up the city's reputation for violent crime had helped him get elected. With opening day of the Century of Progress World's Fair just over six months away, Cermak was under added pressure to make good on his pledge. Now he could chalk up Marcinkiewicz and Majczek as enemy casualties twenty-eight and twenty-nine in the war on crime he had launched back in August.

Among those who were decidedly *not* content was Majczek's mother, Tillie. She knew in her heart that her son was innocent. She and her husband used their life savings to pay their son's lawyer and to appeal the verdict, all to no avail. It was not in her nature to give up, especially where her children were concerned. After some thought, she came up with a plan. It would require hard work, and it might take a very long time for her to reach her goal, but she had to try.

Eleven years later, in October 1944, Karin Walsh, the city editor at the *Chicago Times,* noticed an ad that read: "$5,000 REWARD FOR KILLERS OF OFFICER LUNDY ON DEC. 9, 1932. CALL GRO 1758, 12-7 P.M." She alerted police reporter James McGuire. McGuire called GRO 1758 and reached Tillie Majczek. He listened to her story, made a few notes, and gave the information to Walsh. Walsh assigned writer John J. "Jack" McPhaul to write a "nice little human interest story" based on what McGuire had discovered.

Tillie Majczek, it turned out, had been scrubbing floors on her hands and knees for the past eleven years in order to save up the $5,000. She hoped offering such a large reward would encourage someone to come forward with evidence that would exonerate her son.

As McPhaul later recalled, he "wrote a story making the sixty-year-old scrubwoman the heroine, tossed in a couple of lines from Kipling's *Mother o' Mine* and figured that was that."

It was a slow night, which gave McPhaul time to read a thirty-page document written by the imprisoned Joe Majczek. One claim made by Majczek caused McPhaul to sit up straight in surprise. Majczek insisted that after the verdict in his case, he had been taken to Judge Charles P. Molthrop's chambers, where the judge had stated he believed Majczek was innocent and had promised him a new trial. Not only that, Molthrop had given his word in front of two witnesses.

McPhaul realized that convicts often declare their innocence and complain that they've been railroaded. Still, he felt something was different about this case. Maybe it was because Majczek had used his time in prison so constructively. He had earned his high school diploma, learned typing and shorthand, and had even taken a few college correspondence courses. City editor Walsh agreed that the situation deserved further investigation.

The information McGuire and McPhaul uncovered stunned and sickened them. Although the judge from Majczek's case was no longer alive, they located a witness to the murder, John Zagata. Zagata did not believe Majczek was guilty. He said the judge didn't think so either, and told him he was going to make sure Majczek got a new trial.

McPhaul's research also revealed the troubling circumstances of Majczek's arrest. At first, deli-owner Vera Walush told police she hid in a closet and didn't see the killers clearly. Then, she said she recognized one of them as a young man named Ted. Ted Marcinkiewicz found out the police were looking for him and sought shelter at his friend Joe Majczek's house. Both men were picked up.

In Majczek's document, he wrote that Vera Walush, the state's only witness to identify him, had originally said he was not the killer. She made that assertion twice, but then the police threatened to arrest her for bootlegging if she didn't "cooperate." (Walush was selling liquor from the back room of her deli, a serious violation of the law in 1932.)

When McGuire located Walush in 1944, she would not talk to him. He managed to track down William Fitzgerald, the judge's bailiff at the time. Fitzgerald revealed that the judge had intended to give Majczek a new trial but had been warned that pursuing that avenue would mean the end of his political career. Judge Molthrop's son confirmed that his father thought Majczek was innocent and that the judge was so distressed about the case he paced the floor at night.

McPhaul and McGuire publicized the case in a series of articles for the *Chicago Times*. The newspaper retained State Senator Walker Butler as legal counsel in order to seek Majczek's exoneration. When Butler reviewed the transcript of the original trial, he was appalled. As McPhaul later recalled, Butler stated that "Joe's defense had been so badly botched as to constitute a criminal offense in itself. His counsel had failed to take elementary steps that would have been obvious to a first-year law student." Fitzgerald, the former bailiff, was not surprised. He told McPhaul that Majczek's lawyer had been intoxicated throughout the trial.

A lying witness, a city determined to close the case, a drunk defense attorney—Joe Majczek hadn't stood a chance.

The Illinois Department of Correction considered the evidence, and on August 15, 1945, Governor Dwight H. Green granted

Majczek a full pardon based on innocence. The Illinois legislature voted Majczek $24,000 for the portion of his life that he could never regain. Tillie Majczek had accomplished her goal.

Out west in Los Angeles, producer Darryl F. Zanuck had been following the Majczek story. In the fall of 1947, director Henry Hathaway and a crew of seventy arrived in Chicago. The end result—titled *Call Northside 777*—starred James Stewart as a reporter based on both McPhaul and McGuire. Richard Conte played a character based on Joe Majczek, and Kasia Orzazewski portrayed his mother.

After review, testimony against Ted Marcinkiewicz was deemed unreliable. In 1950 he was exonerated through a state habeas corpus proceeding. The Illinois legislature approved an appropriation of $35,000 for Marcinkiewicz as compensation.

The murder of police officer William D. Lundy was never solved.

NO CURSES IN BASEBALL?

1945

In October 1945, a painting of blue skies graced the cover of *Vogue* magazine, signifying the end of World War II. Atomic power and taxes were the top concerns faced by the United States Congress as it entered the second month of its post-war session. In Hollywood, the Confederation of Studio Unions strike exploded into a full-scale riot as picketers were attacked by what union representatives described as "strikebreakers, Chicago goons and county police."

In the world of baseball, October meant only one thing: the World Series. For Chicago Cubs fans, October 1945 held great promise. After a seven-year absence from the Series, the Cubs were back in the game, battling the Detroit Tigers for the world championship. A victory would give the Cubs a total of three World Series titles. They had last won the Fall Classic in 1907 and 1908.

Back in September, before the Cubs even clinched the National League title, the team announced that it would accept mail order requests for series tickets. Two days later, a *Chicago Daily Tribune* headline proclaimed: "It's a Sellout!" By Friday, October 5, Cubs fans were in high gear. Their team had won two of the first three games of the Series in Detroit. Game four would be played at Wrigley Field in the Windy City.

Chicagoans camped on the sidewalk outside the stadium, braving subfreezing temperatures as they waited for bleacher seats to go on sale. Scalpers made a killing, charging from four to six times the face value for tickets.

The last-minute struggle for admittance to the game did not worry William Sianis. He had purchased two box seats in advance, for which he paid $7.20 apiece. Sianis—nicknamed Billy Goat because of his goatee—was the owner of a tavern on West Madison Street. A Greek immigrant who built his business from the ground up, Billy Goat Sianis was known for his sense of humor. He was fond of telling customers that one of the rooms in his tavern was strictly for VIPs: Very Insecure People.

On Saturday, October 6, the weather forecast was on target: "mostly cloudy with occasional showers." A high of sixty-eight degrees was predicted. Undaunted by the rain, Sianis and his buddy Murphy arrived early at the field, joining a crowd of nearly forty-three thousand. Before taking their seats, the pair strolled onto the playing field. People in the stands pointed and laughed at Murphy, who was wearing a sign that read: "We got Detroit's goat." The sign was especially funny because Murphy was not a typical Cubs fan. He had four legs, large wide-set ears, and horns. He was, without question, a goat.

This fact did not escape the ushers, who escorted Sianis and Murphy to a grandstand aisle. Determined to continue the show, Murphy broke loose and trotted back onto the field. When he posed near the Detroit dugout, fans cheered and flashbulbs popped. Writing the next day for the *Chicago Times,* Gene Kessler noted: "Finally, the goat was permitted to stay in his owner's box after a heated argument. The owner, Billy Sianis, who operates a tavern, argued that he had purchased a box seat for his goat and there was nothing printed on the ticket which said he couldn't use it for an animal."

Murphy's grace period was short-lived. On orders from Cubs owner Philip Knight Wrigley, the ushers ejected Sianis and his rain-soaked goat from the stadium, reportedly because of Murphy's odor. The Cubs lost that game and the next. *Chicago Times* columnist Irv Kupcinet wrote, "After Detroit defeated the Cubs, 8-4 [in game five], Sianis sent P. K. Wrigley this wire: 'Who smells now?'"

When the Cubs won game six on October 8, tying the Series at three to three, suspense peaked in Chicago. Concerning game seven, a *Chicago Times* article announced "Baseball history favors the Chicago Cubs."

But baseball history backed the wrong horse, and Detroit emerged triumphant on October 10 at Wrigley Field.

Had the Cubs won, the 1945 incident involving Billy Goat Sianis and Murphy might have been forgotten. Instead, when the Cubs failed to make it to the World Series for decades afterward, rumors spread that Sianis cursed the Cubs for disrespecting his goat. By one account, the Greek tavern owner vowed in 1945 that the World Series would never be played in Wrigley Field again. Another claimed that Sianis told P. K. Wrigley: "You are never going to go to another World Series." Yet another version had Sianis standing outside the stadium with Murphy on that rainy October day, raising his fist and exclaiming, "The Cubs no win here no more!"

Late in the 1950 season, the *Chicago Sun-Times* printed a letter from Sianis to Wrigley, promising to remove the curse if Wrigley would issue a formal apology. Wrigley complied, but the Cubs kept losing.

The Curse of the Billy Goat became a prominent topic of conversation among Cubs fans around 1969. Sianis passed away in

October 1970, twenty-five years after allegedly cursing the Cubs. In 1972, *Tribune* columnist David Condon wrote: "A quarter-century, plus, has elapsed. [The Series] hasn't returned to Wrigley Field. Billy Goat's hex reaches out from the grave."

To their credit, Cubs fans refused to let the losing seasons get their goat. "Next year," they vowed at the end of each one.

On several occasions the Cubs invited William Sianis's nephew Sam, the new owner of the Billy Goat Tavern, to bring a goat to the field. When this failed to improve the fortune of the Cubs, Sam Sianis suggested that the invitations were ineffective because they were merely publicity stunts. He maintained that the hex could only be lifted if the Cubs opened the stands to goats out of a sincere desire for their presence.

By 1994, the Curse of the Billy Goat had seemingly become as influential as any member of the Cubs team.

"I've got to go down to that tavern and talk to that guy about the goat," said Cubs manager Tom Trebelhorn following a twelve-game losing streak at Wrigley. "We'll let the goat run the bases and water the outfield. We'll let him eat some grass and I'll kiss him. Whatever it takes."

Sam Sianis brought a goat to the stadium on May 4, 1994. The Cubs stopped their streak with a five-to-two victory over the Cincinnati Reds. Unfortunately for Cubs fans, the reversal of fortune did not last long enough to carry the team to the Fall Classic.

In 2004 the Illinois House passed a resolution declaring that "the Cubs Curse shall be no more." That didn't work, either. The Cubs collapsed yet again, losing seven of their last nine games and finishing in third place.

Writing in an Internet blog in January 2007, sports journalist George Castle declared: "There are no curses in baseball, just like there's no crying. The only application of the word can be 'cursed by bad management.'" Castle insisted that The Curse of the Billy Goat was "strictly a media creation."

It's easy to see Castle's point, and yet . . .

The year 2008 marked the one hundredth season since the Cubs last won the World Series. In July, sportswriter Fred Bowen noted: "So far this season the Cubs have been terrific, putting together the best record in the National League. . . . But to win the World Series, even a good team needs to be a little lucky. And luck is something the Chicago Cubs have not had for a long, long time."

Excitement built all through the regular season, as Cubs fans watched their beloved team march to victory in ninety-seven games—the most since 1945. On September 20, 2008, the Cubs officially clinched the Central Division title with a 5-4 win over the St. Louis Cardinals. Chicagoans began to talk about a "Chicago World Series," featuring the Cubs against the White Sox.

Next on the agenda for the Cubs: Win three games out of five over the Los Angeles Dodgers in the first round of the playoffs. Somehow the assignment got scrambled—or maybe the goat ate it. Whatever the reason, the Cubs failed to follow through. Despite Castle's assertion that there are no curses in baseball, curses were heard all over Chicagoland when the Dodgers swept the series, winning the first three games 7-2, 10-3, and 3-1.

"The wind in the Windy City today is caused by the air coming out of the balloon that was the Cubs' golden season," the *Chicago Tribune* intoned mournfully on October 6, 2008.

Maybe next year.

A TALE OF TWO HOFFMANS

1969

Seventy-four-year-old Julius Jennings Hoffman was a federal court judge. Just over five feet four inches tall and bald, he typically wore custom-made suits and gold cuff links. His admirers described him as punctilious and dedicated—"imbued with the Protestant ethic." A detractor referred to him as "a perfect representative of a class of dinosaurs that is vengefully striking out against the future."

Abbott H. (better known as Abbie) Hoffman, age thirty-three, stood five feet seven inches tall. A wealth of dark, tangled hair crowned his head. He typically wore a headband, beads, and colorful shirts with jeans. A leader of the Youth International Party (better known as the Yippies), he was a self-proclaimed "orphan of America." Journalist Jack Newfield labeled him "a pure Marxist-Lennonist—Harpo Marx and John Lennon."

When the paths of the two Hoffmans crossed in 1969 in Chicago, their differences took on a significance greater than they could have imagined.

As the date of the 1968 National Democratic Convention approached, Abbie Hoffman and his fellow Yippies decided to stage a Festival of Life in Chicago to counteract what they called the "Convention of Death."

"Join us in Chicago in August for an international festival of youth, music, and theater," read a flyer announcing their plans. "Come all you rebels, youth spirits, rock minstrels, truth-seekers, peacock-freaks, poets, barricade-jumpers, dancers, lovers and artists!"

Opposition to the war in Vietnam motivated many of the demonstrators but, as historian David Farber pointed out: "The conflict was over how the American political system worked and over how Americans found meaning in their lives. . . . The demonstrators who came to Chicago did so in order to confront a national symbol."

City officials denied a Yippie application for a permit to sleep in Chicago parks, but on the night of August 25, 1968, people in Lincoln Park refused to obey the city's 11:00 p.m. curfew. Police tried to drive them out with clubs.

Over the next several days, an estimated eighty-nine million Americans watched on television as the brutality in Chicago escalated. Armed with mace and tear gas, the police went head-to-head with demonstrators who countered with sticks, rocks, bottles, chunks of concrete, and stink bombs. Each attack generated an equally violent or more violent response from the other side. On August 28, National Guard troops arrived.

Chicago Tribune headlines kept up with the action: "Cops, Hippies War in Street" (August 29); "Cops Pressed Beyond Limit, They Assert: Charge News Reports Favor Demonstrators," "2,000 Flee to Park in Tear Gas Attacks" (August 30).

On March 20, 1969, Abbie Hoffman, Tom Hayden, and six other individuals were arraigned in the United States District Court for the Northern District of Illinois. They were charged with conspiracy to cross state lines "with the intent to incite, organize, promote, encourage, participate in, and carry out a riot" during the Democratic Convention. In addition to conspiracy, six of the defendants were charged with inciting violence, and two were charged with teaching others how to make incendiary devices.

The trial began on September 24 in Judge Julius Hoffman's oak-paneled courtroom in Chicago's shiny new Federal Building. Three of the defendants—Rennie Davis, Dave Dellinger, and Tom Hayden—were key members of "the Mobe," the National Mobilization Committee to End the War in Vietnam. Abbie Hoffman and Jerry Rubin were Yippies. John Froines, a chemist, was a member of Students for a Democratic Society (SDS). Lee Weiner was a Ph.D. sociology student.

An eighth defendant, Bobby Seale, was chairman of the Black Panther Party. Seale's case was eventually separated from the others, and the Chicago Eight became the Chicago Seven.

Most people who were acquainted with the Chicago Seven knew the conspiracy charge was a stretch. The Yippies and the Mobe were too diverse in their political views to actually conspire about much of anything.

"Conspiracy?" Abbie Hoffman said. "Hell, we couldn't agree on lunch."

They couldn't agree on how to handle themselves during the trial, either. As Rubin put it: "The yippies . . . were on trial to have a good time, and to use the media and guerrilla theater, humor, fun and rage to expose Amerikan [sic] injustice to young people." In fact, as Abbie Hoffman explained during the trial, the so-called Youth International Party never existed. It was a "put-on" for the media.

In contrast, according to Rubin, Hayden and the Mobe felt it was most important to "win the case with the jury . . . through rational arguments and good behavior," and get the trial over with as soon as possible. "Such political differences made it impossible for us to live together," Rubin noted. "In fact we relished our time apart."

It was easy to predict that the two Hoffmans would clash. The trial transcript from the first day contains the following words from the judge: "The jury is directed to disregard the kiss thrown by the defendant Hoffman and the defendant is directed not to do that sort of thing again."

At first, Abbie Hoffman referred to the judge as his "illegitimate father." Later, he announced that he would no longer use the last name Hoffman. Complaining about one of the judge's rulings, Abbie Hoffman declared that it was the worst he'd heard "in all my years on the witness stand."

Julius Hoffman matched Abbie Hoffman's complaint with one of his own: "Never in my fifty years in court have I heard so much obscenity as I've heard during this trial." Abbie Hoffman was ready for him: "Your idea of justice is the only obscenity in the room, Julie," he said.

Abbie Hoffman's antics included showing up in court wearing black judicial robes under his overcoat. He winked, sighed, gasped, stretched, waved, and "made eyes" at the judge and jury throughout the five-month trial.

Not to be outdone, Judge Hoffman repeatedly used sarcasm and ridicule to put the defendants and their attorneys in their place. After a ruling on hearsay grounds, defense attorney William Kunstler said, "I just don't understand it." Judge Hoffman replied: "You will have to see a lawyer, Mr. Kunstler, if you don't understand it."

On February 18, 1970, after deliberating four days, the jury acquitted all defendants on the conspiracy charge. The five defendants charged with having an intent to incite a riot while crossing state lines were found guilty. On February 20, Judge Hoffman sentenced them to five years in prison and fines of $5,000 each plus "the costs of prosecution."

Although it looked like Julius Hoffman had won the "Battle of the Hoffmans," his victory was only temporary. In November 1972, the Seventh Circuit Court of Appeals reversed all of the convictions. The ruling noted: "The district judge's deprecatory and often antagonistic attitude toward the defense is evident in the record from the very beginning. . . . We conclude that the demeanor of the judge and prosecutors would require reversal if other errors did not."

Eleven years later, Julius Jennings Hoffman died at his home in Chicago, a few days before he was to celebrate his eighty-eighth birthday. Abbie Hoffman was outbid in his attempt to buy the judge's mahogany gavel at auction.

Abbie Hoffman died in April 1989 in his home in Pennsylvania from the combined effects of phenobarbital and alcohol. His brother Jack described him as being nearly broke. "He gave just about everything away," he said. "He didn't die with a Rolex. He died with a full heart."

A NEW FACE

1984

"Start the Day with a New Face" suggested the headline of the ad in the *Chicago Tribune.*

In January 1984, when the ad ran, most Chicagoans would rather have started the day with new weather. The previous month had gone on record as the coldest December in Chicago's history. The temperature had remained below zero for twelve straight days. On Christmas Eve it dipped to twenty-five degrees below.

Among those who looked forward to warmer days was one of the city's newest residents.

"This cold was awesome," she recalled years later. "It was serious cold. I thought I was delirious in the streets!"

Although the young woman had been born in Mississippi and lived much of her life in Tennessee, she was no stranger to winter weather. She had also lived in Wisconsin and Maryland. But her first week in Chicago made her revise her definition of "cold."

"I remember walking to the corner and getting blown down by the wind, and I said, 'Well, this is a sign I'm supposed to go back to the hotel!'"

Fortunately, the twenty-nine-year-old woman had formed a bond with Chicago three months earlier. "I set foot in this city," she said of the September visit, "and just walking down the street, it was like roots, like the motherland. I knew I belonged here."

December's chilly reception did not destroy that feeling, nor did the awareness of other challenges she was likely to face in the Windy City. On January 1, 1984, she started working for Chicago's ABC affiliate, WLS-TV. Hers was the "new face" advertised in the newspaper. The ad went on to exclaim:

"Say hello to AM Chicago's fresh new hostess.

She's vivacious. Interesting. Exciting. And fun.

She's Oprah Winfrey. And you're gonna love her."

A.M. Chicago, which was patterned after *A.M. America* (ABC's answer to the *Today* show), had premiered in 1975. Likeable hosts and uncontroversial subject matter—described by one writer as "a little chitchat, a little fashion, a little personality stuff, a little cooking, a little homemaking"—had not earned it high ratings.

In 1984, the undisputed ruler of the talk-show business was Phil Donahue, aka the "owner" of daytime television. His show had moved from Ohio to Chicago in 1974. One of the challenges Oprah Winfrey faced in her new job (along with harsh Midwestern winters) was direct competition from Donahue. His program aired in the same time slot as *A.M. Chicago.*

The day she was hired, WLS general manger Dennis Swanson told her, "We know you can't beat Donahue. We just want to go up in the ratings."

Winfrey respected Donahue but was not overly awed by him. Her Baltimore show, *People Are Talking,* had had a higher rating than his. There was room for hope.

Aside from winter weather and Donahue, Winfrey was keenly aware of other battles she would have to wage in Chicago.

"Everybody, with the exception of my best friend, told me it wouldn't work," she confided years later. "They said I was black, female, and overweight. They said Chicago is a racist city and the talk-show formula was on its way out."

Discouraged only slightly by the naysayers, Winfrey reminded herself that Chicago had elected its first woman mayor, Jane Byrne, in 1979 and its first black mayor, Harold Washington, in 1983. Again, room for hope. In addition, both Dennis Swanson and producer Debra DiMaio had confidence that Winfrey would succeed.

Swanson was a burly ex-Marine whose huge desk displayed a piece of stone inscribed: "Be reasonable. Do it my way." His arrival in Chicago from Los Angeles in July 1983 had prompted a bit of a shake-up at WLS. His reaction upon seeing a tape of Winfrey on *People Are Talking* was immediate and positive: "That young woman was sensational," he said later. "I brought in all my program people, and they agreed. So I called her. When you've looked at as many audition tapes as I have, hers just jumped out of the stack."

Winfrey was astonished when Swanson told her he was concerned about how she would handle being famous.

"You really think it will go that well?" she asked.

"I would bet on it," he said.

After signing a four-year contract with WLS-TV for $200,000 a year, Winfrey leaped right into the fray. On New Year's Eve 1983, she was introduced to the city at the traditional State Street celebration. On New Year's Day she was welcomed to town by a parade featuring a marching band, color guard, and cheerleaders from area schools. On January 2, she hosted an hour-long "Rose Bowl extravaganza."

Within a few weeks, *A.M. Chicago* passed Donahue's show in the ratings. In March, Winfrey hosted a dialogue with Ku Klux Klan members. Her viewers numbered 265,000, compared to 147,230 for Donahue.

"Oprah hit Chicago like a bucket of cold water," Swanson recalled. "It was amazing. There was no gradual build. We went from last in the time period to number one in about four weeks. She just took over the town."

No one was more shocked than Winfrey herself. "That very first show there I am standing out in the middle of State Street with a marching band and a Jheri curl," she recalled later. "How in the world did an overweight Jheri curl black woman become successful enough to beat Donahue? I don't know."

When she first came to Chicago, Winfrey imagined that it would take about a year before she would be recognized as she walked down the street. On March 13, 1984, television critic Jon Anderson wrote: "On- and off-screen, her presence is undeniable, despite her short Chicago track record: three months. She is greeted by strangers on the street, recognized in restaurants and once was driven to work by a policeman when she was late and couldn't get a cab."

Winfrey's personality was engaging, unorthodox, booming, effervescent, and—according to biographer Norman King—"vulnerable in that peculiarly aggressive Oprah Winfrey way." Biographer Robert Waldron wrote: "She behaved like the down-to-earth, gregarious next-door neighbor you could trust to spill your deepest, darkest secrets to over a cup of coffee and a slice of pound cake."

Winfrey's blend of sass, sensibility, and sensationalism appealed to the people of Chicago, a "real city," as Rudyard Kipling called it, adding: "The other places do not count." Winfrey herself referred to Chicago as "a more polished New York."

In December 1984, one year after a newspaper ad encouraged readers to "start the day with a new face," *Newsweek* pronounced Oprah Winfrey the hottest press star in Chicago.

Racism, sexism, weight issues, Donahue—none of it seemed to matter. Seven months into Winfrey's run, *A.M. Chicago* was expanded from thirty minutes to a full hour. In 1985 the show was renamed *The Oprah Winfrey Show*. It went national in 1986.

For all practical purposes, Winfrey's rise to fame took place in Chicago: the town that felt like "the motherland" to her on her very first visit. Since then, she has also managed to make her mark as a movie actress, starring in Steven Spielberg's adaptation of Alice Walker's novel, *The Color Purple*.

She formed Harpo Productions, Inc. (the name of the company is Oprah spelled backwards) and purchased a building in the West Loop in 1989 to house her offices and studio. Winfrey has also been an executive producer for a number of made-for-television movies such as *Tuesdays with Morrie* and *Their Eyes Were Watching God*, along with the feature film *The Great Debaters*.

In 2001, *AdWeek* magazine named Winfrey's magazine—*O, The Oprah Magazine*—Start-Up of the Year. *Advertising Age* awarded it Best Magazine of the Year and Best Launch of the Year honors. Additional awards soon followed.

To kick off her television program's twenty-third season in 2008, Winfrey welcomed more than one hundred and fifty American athletes who performed at the Olympic Games in Beijing, China. Fans began lining up at 6:00 a.m. Saturday, August 30, for a chance to snag free tickets to the September 2 taping of the show. At 11:50 a.m., the line stretched out of Chicago's Millennium Park onto Randolph Street and continued about six blocks across the Columbus Drive bridge. Many wanted tickets so that they could see the Olympians, but many just wanted to see Winfrey.

"I love Oprah," said a Chicago native standing in line. "I didn't even know who else was going to be on the show until now."

Winfrey planned the show not only to honor the athletes but to boost Chicago's bid for the 2016 Olympics. As the *Chicago Tribune* put it, "A Winfrey endorsement can be gold."

LAUNCHING A CAREER

1990

The early morning sky was still dark as Thomas O'Malley walked to his van. The air was so frosty it hurt to inhale. The wind stung his face. *Chicago in February,* he thought. *There's nothing like it.*

At the moment, about eight inches of snow covered the ground. O'Malley hoped temperatures wouldn't dip the way they had two months ago. December 21, 1989, had made weather history, breaking records that had stood for more than a century. A low of fourteen degrees below zero was documented along with a low maximum temperature of zero.

Tall and white-haired, O'Malley had twinkling blue eyes that could turn steely gray in seconds when someone irritated him. He looked every bit like the police officer he had once been. These days, his job was considerably less dangerous. When asked to describe his work, he simply said, "I'm a driver."

O'Malley's current assignment was a pleasant one, despite the need to start his day before dawn. After a quick stop at a bakery, where he picked up donuts and coffee to go, he headed for the

Belden-Stratford, a turn-of-the-century, fourteen-story structure nestled in Lincoln Park. Residents and guests of the Belden-Stratford enjoyed panoramic views of Lake Michigan, the Lincoln Park Zoo, and the downtown Chicago skyline.

O'Malley entered the ornate lobby with its oak-paneled walls, oil paintings, hand-woven tapestries, and giant palms. He crossed the white marble floor to the front desk, where he placed a telephone call to a corner apartment on the top floor.

Within twenty minutes, he was driving up the western shore of Lake Michigan with his charges—an unusually bright, personable nine-year-old boy and his father. O'Malley's route took him through Evanston and the campus of Northwestern University, then through several affluent suburbs. This morning, the final destination was New Trier High School in Winnetka, about nineteen miles north of downtown Chicago.

In the parking lot at New Trier, the boy climbed onto O'Malley's lap for a ritual they performed nearly every day. While O'Malley retained control over the gas pedal and brake, the boy steered the van around the lot at about two miles per hour, a huge grin on his face.

Inside the building, locker-lined hallways and polished linoleum floors confirmed that the place had at one time been a high school. Now, instead of students hastening to class or lounging against door frames, O'Malley saw people gliding along on bicycles, scooters, or in-line skates. Some of them could have been high-school age, but most seemed older.

He escorted the boy and his father to the gymnasium. It looked very different from any high school gymnasium O'Malley had ever seen. One corner more nearly resembled the messy basement of a typical suburban home, complete with a dress form, Halloween skulls, an old football helmet, and a croquet set.

The boy—called Mack by those who knew him well—took a quick look around the gym, then retreated to a cement-walled room furnished with chairs, couches, rugs, and lamps. Connected to that room was a bathroom and a standard classroom, including desks, blackboards, and bookcases for his required three hours of instruction per day.

A young man wearing blue jeans, a sweatshirt, and well-worn sneakers appeared in the doorway. "Are you ready?" he asked.

The young man was Chris Columbus, thirty-two-year-old director of *Heartbreak Hotel* (1988) and *Adventures in Babysitting* (1987). The boy was Macaulay Culkin, a nine-year-old actor who had appeared in Off-Broadway shows somewhere between ages four and six, and in his first film—*Rocket Gibraltar* with Burt Lancaster—at age eight. As a member of the film's Transportation Department, O'Malley was responsible for driving Culkin and his father, Kit, wherever they needed to go. Kit Culkin referred to the former police officer as "the right honorable Thomas Patrick Francis O'Malley."

Back in January of 1990, the *Chicago Tribune* had alerted would-be actors with blurbs like the following: "Opportunity knocks . . . 1 p.m. Saturday at 700 S. Desplaines St. They need people for an airport scene in 'Home Alone,' which begins filming here next month. Bring a photo or snapshot and two forms of ID."

Home Alone's scriptwriter, John Hughes, was well known to Chicagoans. The forty-year-old writer-director-producer owned and operated Hughes Entertainment in Chicago. His credits included *Sixteen Candles* (1984); *The Breakfast Club* (1985); *Ferris Bueller's Day Off* (1986); *Pretty in Pink* (1986); *Planes, Trains & Automobiles* (1987); and *Uncle Buck* (1989).

In *Home Alone*, Culkin played Kevin McCallister, an eight-year-old boy who is accidentally left behind when his wealthy family takes off for a Christmas vacation in France. At first, Kevin is thrilled to have the house (and his life) to himself. His joy is soon dampened—not only by the fact that he misses his family, but by the appearance of two idiotic burglars who are robbing homes all along Kevin's street.

A home on Lincoln Avenue in Winnetka was used for exterior shots of the impressive McCallister abode. Other locations included Grace Episcopal Church in Oak Park, Grand Food Center in Winnetka, Haven Middle School in Evanston, and Trinity Methodist Church in Wilmette.

Although Chicago was given a prominent role in *Home Alone,* the city did not take direction very well. When the producers requested snow for their holiday story, Chicago shrugged its Big Shoulders and said, "Sorry, no can do." Other movie companies filming that winter had been forced to use instant potato flakes. As spring approached, the *Home Alone* team faced the fact that it would have to do the same.

"Giant ice machines and snow blowers were therefore brought in," Kit Culkin divulged. "They blew ice and snow simply everywhere, and (of course) with no low temperature to support this assault, wound up making a perfectly muddy mess of the area." The instant potato flakes mixed with the mud, creating "potato mud soup . . . a dark and creamy *vichyssoise.*"

The cast and crew persevered, wrapping up production in May 1990. The tagline for publicity purposes was "A family comedy without the family." Movie posters featured Culkin with his eyes wide, hands to his face, and mouth opened in a scream.

Released in November, *Home Alone* received an interesting mixture of reviews, which included such descriptors as: "generally engaging," "excessively sadistic," "an unnecessary, marginally funny movie with a serious lack of credibility and a banal message," "surprisingly enjoyable," "silly and cartoonish," "a nice breath of fresh air," and "so freaking fluffy it makes me retch."

Looking back in August 1991, David Lyman of Scripps-Howard News Service observed: "Only the foolhardy or the prescient would have predicted *Home Alone* would be a monstrous hit. . . . After all, it was a modest entertainment geared to a kids' audience."

Whatever the critics may have thought or said about *Home Alone,* movie-goers queued up by the thousands to see it. The film grossed more than $285 million in the United States alone, making it one of the highest grossing movies of all time. Without question, *Home Alone* launched Macaulay Culkin's career as a film star. The little boy who rode along the western shore of Lake Michigan in Thomas O'Malley's van became a superstar with a fleet of limousines at his service. Paid $250,000 for *Home Alone,* Culkin earned well over a million dollars each for subsequent films.

SPITTING IMAGES

2004

One summer afternoon in early summer 2003, a young woman at the School of the Art Institute of Chicago (SAIC) picked up the telephone and started to place a call. She hesitated, frowned, and replaced the receiver in its cradle. This wasn't going to be easy. Would anyone understand what she was asking them to do? And if they understood, would they trust her? She had nothing to show them as an example of what they were getting into.

With a sigh, she picked up the receiver again and punched in the first telephone number on her list. Her assignment was to sign up a thousand people for this project, and she had to start somewhere.

Looking back more than a year and a half later, the young woman—Mery Palarea-Lobos, a graduate of the SAIC's arts administration program—could only shake her head and laugh.

"I started with community-based arts groups," she told reporter Emily Nunn of the *Chicago Tribune*. "It was actually very funny. They were like: 'No, we don't participate in that kind of thing.' . . . I won't say all of them, but I didn't get a great response."

She had more luck when she contacted social-service organizations, immigrant organizations, and consulates.

"We didn't really know what they were talking about initially," admitted Linh Pham, a staff member from the Chinese Mutual Aid Association. "But we were like, 'Oh, our picture taken? OK.'"

Palarea-Lobos was eventually able to locate more than eight hundred Chicagoans who shared Linh Pham's sense of adventure and were willing to come to the SAIC for a photo shoot.

"We got first-generation Chicagoans, brand-new immigrants, people whose families have been in Chicago for as long as they can remember," Palarea-Lobos told the *Tribune*. "And we got a pretty good range of cultural and ethnic backgrounds."

They arrived at the SAIC in a steady stream seven days a week for three weeks during the summer of 2003. One at a time, they were ushered into a studio and seated in a dentist's chair. For five to ten minutes, they were asked to stare, look relaxed, smile, and purse their lips as if blowing out a birthday candle. Children were sometimes asked to make a "fish face." A videographer using a top-of-the-line high-definition camcorder taped each individual's personal "movie."

In many cases, the models—ranging in age from seven to eighty—didn't fully grasp how the images would be used. That became clear in the summer of 2004, when they visited the latest jewel in Chicago's crown: a twenty-five-acre phenomenon called Millennium Park.

Built on a roof over underground parking and commuter rail tracks in the Chicago Loop area, the park was created by an alliance of planners, engineers, architects, artists, and landscape designers. Years in the making, it eventually boasted a music pavilion, a theater, elaborate gardens, an ice skating rink, a 925-foot-long winding pedestrian bridge, and two amazing works of public art.

One of the artworks—*Cloud Gate* by British artist Anish Kapoor—was a highly polished reflective steel sculpture intended to resemble a drop of mercury hovering at the point of landing on a plaza of the park.

The park's other extraordinary work of art—*The Crown Fountain*—featured the faces of Chicagoans who posed for the SAIC. Designed by Spanish artist Jaume Plensa, the fountain was named in honor of the Lester Crown family. The Crowns selected Plensa as the artist and funded the project. Although *The Crown Fountain* was an appropriate name, it didn't convey all that Plensa's creation was.

ARCHI-TECH magazine provided a detailed description:

> [T]wo fifty-foot towers facing each other at opposite
> ends of a reflecting pool. . . . Each is made of glass
> blocks protecting an LED screen that randomly displays
> a person's face, a nature scene, or a solid color. Then,
> water rushes down from the top of the structure, wash-
> ing away the face, and another picture appears. Water
> continuously falls from the sides and back of each
> tower.

Writing for the *Chicago Tribune* in 2007, Ellen Fox commented that Chicagoans had lovingly retitled the fountain: "The Big Videos of the Faces that Spit Water Sometimes and the Kids All Run Around In It."

Fox's title was offered in jest but was not inaccurate. The videos were indeed "big"—twenty-three feet wide and fifty feet high, nearly twice as tall as the average movie screen.

"We had to stretch [the models'] heads like taffy," said John Manning in an interview published in the *Tribune*. Manning, a faculty member at the SAIC, was part of a team that pulled the project together over a period of two and a half years. "Each face had to fit the building. We had to make sure that the eyes were always in the same place on the fountain for each person." Hence the use of a dentist's chair, which could be raised and lowered while the camcorder remained in the same position.

Fox's "Faces that Spit Water Sometimes" also rang true. As Manning noted: "The mouth, especially, had to be in precisely the same place because there's a 6-inch nozzle that shoots the water out. We call it 'the gargoyle effect.'"

In their role as gargoyles, the SAIC models carried on a respected tradition. During the Middle Ages and Renaissance, fountains incorporated the faces of gargoyles, and water spouted from their mouths. This homage to days gone by was deliberate on Plensa's part.

"All of us, we have two sides," Plensa said, "the daylight side, and the freak side. . . . And those huge faces, the gargoyles become these grotesque parts of ourselves, but that is also the most beautiful part of art, when we are out of control. When they spout water from their mouth, they are giving us life, and that is very beautiful for me."

In addition to the original group of models, three hundred more people were eventually videotaped, including workers who participated in building the fountain. Photographer and SAIC faculty member Allan Labb remarked that after the filming was over and everyone knew how the video was being used, he received phone calls from Chicagoans clamoring to have their "spitting images" incorporated into *The Crown Fountain*.

According to author Timothy J. Gilfoyle, Plensa agreed to determine the images for only the initial two years of the fountain's life. Future generations will be able to make The Crown Fountain their own, ensuring that it remains a fresh and relevant part of Chicago's ongoing history.

Fox's title for the fountain ended with "and the Kids All Run Around In It." Right again. On summer afternoons, as many as three hundred children have been observed splashing, kicking, crawling, or wallowing in a quarter of an inch of water in the reflecting pool. Plensa insists that the pool, which is more than two hundred and thirty feet long and forty-eight feet wide, is not a pool, just a "very thin skin of water."

Plensa's goal was to create not a sculpture but an environment, to take a space and transform it, to regenerate an area. He succeeded on all counts.

In the winter, when Chicago's climate requires that the fountain be waterless, it continues to "speak" in what art critic Alan G. Artner described as "the language of a '70s light show and Times Square jumbotron."

Writing back in 1883, Mark Twain seemed to understand what Chicago was and what it could become. He wrote: "It is hopeless for the occasional visitor to try to keep up with Chicago—she outgrows his prophesies faster than he can make them. She is always a novelty, for she is never the Chicago you saw when you passed through the last time." The changing faces on *The Crown Fountain* bear witness to the truth of his statement.

CHICAGO FACTS AND TRIVIA

- Chicago is the largest city in Illinois and the third largest city in the United States.

- Chicago was laid out in 1830, incorporated as a village in 1833, and incorporated as a city in 1837.

- Etymology experts continue to debate the origin of the word *Chicago* and its meaning. It seems likely that the Native American version of the name pertained to an area rich in a kind of wild garlic, onion, or leek.

- Researchers have learned that Chicago's nickname "The Windy City" appeared as early as 1860. Etymologist Barry Popik located an article in the July 4, 1860, Milwaukee (WI) *Daily Sentinel* that mentioned "Chicago, the windy city of the West." Ohio newspapers used the term "Windy City" to refer to Chicago repeatedly during the 1870s. The term was used both literally (as a reference to gusty winds) and figuratively (as a derisive reference to pretentious bragging on the part of Chicagoans). Credit for either coining or popularizing the nickname has also been given to Charles Dana, editor of the *New York Sun*, who supposedly used it in 1890. However, Dana's alleged words have never been found. There is no proof that he ever wrote them.

- Chicago has numerous other nicknames, including City of the Big Shoulders, The Prairie City, Gem of the Prairie, Hog Butcher to the World, Packingtown, and Second City.

- Chicago's city seal reads "Urbs in Horto," which means "City in a Garden" in Latin.

- Chicago's motto "I Will" was coined after the Great Chicago Fire in 1871.

- The city flower is the chrysanthemum. The official bird is the peregrine falcon.

- The Chicago Municipal flag was designed by Wallace Rice and adopted in 1917. It consists of two blue horizontal stripes on a field of white. Between the two blue stripes are four red, six-pointed stars arranged in a horizontal row. The two blue stripes represent Lake Michigan and the Chicago River. The three white stripes represent the North Side, West Side, and South Side of Chicago. Each star represents a significant event in Chicago's history: Fort Dearborn, the Great Chicago Fire, and the World's Fairs of 1893 and 1933. The points on the fourth star refer to Chicago's status as the World's Third Largest City, Chicago's Latin Motto (Urbs in Horto—City in a garden), Chicago's "I Will" Motto, and Chicago's identity as Great Central Marketplace, Wonder City, and Convention City.

- Famous Chicagoans (born in Chicago) include politicians Hillary Rodham Clinton, "Bathhouse John" Coughlin, Richard J. Daley, Carter Henry Harrison II, Michael "Hinky Dink" Kenna, and Harold Washington; judges Mary Bartelme, Arthur J. Goldberg, John Marshall Harlan II, and Julius J. Hoffman; actors Gillian Anderson, John Belushi, Harrison Ford, Joe Mantegna, Clayton Moore, Martin Mull, Gloria Swanson, Laurence Turead ("Mr. T"), Raquel Welch, and Robin Williams; social reformer Louise DeKoven Bowen; authors Edgar Rice Burroughs, Raymond Chandler, Michael Crichton, John Dos Passos, James T.

Farrell, John Gunther, Ernest Hemingway, Meyer Levin, Shel Silverstein, and Irving Wallace; musicians Paul Butterfield, Bud Freeman, Benny Goodman, Steve Goodman, Gene Krupa, and Curtis Mayfield; singers Sam Cooke, Johanna Meier, Anita O'Day, and Mel Tormé; choreographer/film director Bob Fosse; football coach George Halas; political activist Fred Hampton; playwrights Kenneth Sawyer Goodman, Lorraine Hansberry, David Mamet, and Melvin Van Peebles; astronomers George Ellery Hale and J. Allen Hynek; labor activist James C. Petrillo; architect Howard Van Doren Shaw; puppeteer Burr Tillstrom; television personality Pat Sajak; entrepreneur/civic leader Charles H. Wacker; theatrical producer Florenz Ziegfeld; comedians Jack Benny, George Gobel, and Bob Newhart; motion picture director Vincent Minnelli; television commentator John Chancellor; psychologist Carl R. Rogers; Olympic gold medalist Dorothy Hamill; broadcasting executive William S. Paley; and composer Quincy Jones.

- Chicago was home to the world's first skyscraper. Depending on your definition of "skyscraper," it was either the nine-story Home Insurance Building erected on LaSalle Street in 1885 or the sixteen-story Monadnock Building erected on West Jackson Boulevard in 1891.

- World-renowned architect Frank Lloyd Wright built his first house in the Oak Park neighborhood of Chicago in 1889.

- To reduce the epidemics of diseases caused by poor sewers, the flow of the Chicago River was reversed in 1900.

- Walt Disney was born in Chicago in 1901. His father, Elias, worked as a carpenter on the World's Columbian Exposition.

- Major League Baseball's first All-Star Game was played on July 6, 1933, at Chicago's Comiskey Park.

- The first hospital blood bank in the United States was established in 1937 in Chicago by Bernard Fantus, director of therapeutics at the Cook County Hospital. Fantus also originated the term "blood bank."

- Movies filmed in Chicago include *North by Northwest* (1959), *The Sting* (1973), *The Blues Brothers* (1979), *Risky Business* (1982), *The Untouchables* (1986), *Uncle Buck* (1989), *Home Alone* (1990), *The Jackal* (1996), *The Watcher* (1999), *I-Robot* (2003), and *The Dark Knight* (2007).

- Television shows filmed in Chicago include *Route 66, Night Stalker, The Bob Newhart Show, Good Times, Hill Street Blues, Real People, T.J. Hooker, Knight Rider, The David Letterman Show, Unsolved Mysteries, Wheel of Fortune, America's Funniest People, ER, Chicago Hope, The Bernie Mack Show, Politically Incorrect, Oprah Winfrey Show, Good Morning America, Martha Stewart Living, The West Wing, American Idol, Prison Break, The Apprentice, The O'Reilly Factor,* and *Beauty and the Geek.*

BIBLIOGRAPHY

GENERAL SOURCES

Algren, Nelson. *Chicago: City on the Make.* Fiftieth Anniversary Edition. Newly Annotated by David Schmittgens and Bill Savage. Chicago: The University of Chicago Press, 2001.

Andreas, A. T. *History of Chicago from the Earliest Period to the Present Time in Three Volumes.* Chicago: A. T. Andreas, Publisher, 1884.

Chicago Days: 150 Defining Moments in the Life of a Great City by the staff of the *Chicago Tribune.* Edited by Stevenson Swanson. Wheaton, Illinois: Cantigny First Division Foundation, 1997.

Cromie, Robert. *A Short History of Chicago.* San Francisco: Lexikos, 1984.

The Electronic Encyclopedia of Chicago © 2005 Chicago Historical Society. *The Encyclopedia of Chicago* © 2004 The Newberry Library. www.encyclopedia.chicagohistory.org/ (accessed on January 27, 2008).

Miller, Donald L. *City of the Century.* New York: Simon & Schuster, 1996.

Pierce, Bessie Louise. *A History of Chicago, Volume III: The Rise of a Modern City, 1871–1893.* New York: Alfred A. Knopf, 1957.

Sawyers, June Skinner. *Chicago Portraits: Biographies of 250 Famous Chicagoans.* Chicago: Loyola University Press, 1991.

———. *Chicago Sketches: Urban Tales, Stories, and Legends from Chicago History.* Chicago: Loyola University Press, 1995.

Spinney, Robert G. *City of Big Shoulders: A History of Chicago.*
DeKalb: Northern Illinois University Press, 2000.

Putting Down Roots

Davey, Monica. "Tribute to Chicago Icon and Enigma," *New York Times,* June 25, 2003, p. A16.

Leeds, Patricia. "Du Sable's Pioneer Role is Recalled," *Chicago Tribune,* July 15, 1976, p. N2.

Leonard, William. "Grave of Chicago Pioneer Dedication," *Chicago Tribune,* October 27, 1968, p. A14.

Meehan, Thomas A. "Jean Baptiste Point du Sable, The First Chicagoan," *Journal of the Illinois State Historical Society* LVI, no. 3, Autumn 1963, pp. 439–53.

Quaife, Milo Milton. *Chicago and the Old Northwest, 1673–1835.* University of Chicago Press, 1913.

Swenson, John F. "Point de Sable, Jean Baptiste," *Early Chicago.* www.earlychicago.com/encyclopedia.php?letter=P (accessed June 10, 2008).

Ordered to Evacuate

The Fort Dearborn Massacre: Written in 1814 by Lieutenant Linai T. Helm, with Letters and Narratives of Contemporary Interest. Edited by Nelly Kinzie Gordon. Chicago: Rand McNally & Company, 1912.

Indians of the Chicago Area, 2nd ed. Compiled and edited by Terry Straus. Chicago: NAES College Press, 1990.

Kinzie, Juliette Augusta Magill. *Wau-bun: The Early Day in the Northwest.* Philadelphia: J. B. Lippincott & Co., 1873.

Kirkland, Joseph. *The Chicago Massacre of 1812.* Chicago: The Dibble Publishing Company, 1893.

Quaife, Milo Milton. *Chicago and the Old Northwest, 1673–1835.* University of Chicago Press, 1913.

Farewell to *Eshegago*

Clifton, James A. "Chicago, September 14, 1833: The Last Great Indian Treaty in the Old Northwest," *Chicago History: The Magazine of the Chicago Historical Society* IX, no. 2, Summer 1980, pp. 86–96.

Latrobe, Charles Joseph. *The Rambler in North America,* 2 vols. London: R. B. Seeley, 1835.

Perrot, Donald, Intertribal Spiritual Leader, Prairie Band Potawatomi Interpreter/Translator. E-mail correspondence, June 2008.

Quaife, Milo Milton. *Chicago and the Old Northwest 1673–1835.* University of Chicago Press, 1913.

Strong, William Duncan. *The Indians of the Chicago Region.* Chicago Field Museum of Natural History, 1926.

Treaty with the Chippewa, Ottawa, and Potawatomi Indians, 1833. In General Records of the U.S. Government, Record Group 11, Ratified Indian Treaties (M668), National Archives, Washington, D.C. Included in Charles J. Kappler, ed., *Indian Treaties 1778–1883.* Reprint edition: Interland Publishing Company, 1975.

Vogel, Virgil. "The Tribes," *Indians of the Chicago Area,* 2nd ed. Compiled and edited by Terry Straus. Chicago: NAES College Press, 1990.

Up, Up, and Hooray!

Cain, Louis P. "Raising and Watering a City: Ellis Sylvester Chesbrough and Chicago's First Sanitation System," *Technology and Culture: The International Quarterly of the Society for History of Technology* 13, no. 3, July 1972.

A Century of Progress in Water Works, 1833-1933. Prepared by Bureau of Engineering, Department of Public Works, City of Chicago. Chicago: The Fred J. Ringley Company, Printers, 1933.

Chicago Daily Tribune articles, January 1855–July 1861.

Macrae, David. *The Americans at Home.* New York: E. P. Dutton & Co., Inc., 1952.

A Party in the Great Wigwam

Chicago Press and Tribune articles, March–May 1860.

Hesseltine, William B., ed. *Three against Lincoln: Murat Halstead Reports the Caucuses of 1860,* 1st ed. Baton Rouge: Louisiana State University Press, 1960. www.questia.com/ PM.qst?a=o&d=11242325 (accessed March 17, 2008).

Ray, P. Orman. *The Convention that Nominated Lincoln; an Address Delivered before the Chicago Historical Society on May 18, 1916, the Fifty-sixth Anniversary of Lincoln's Nomination for the Presidency.* University of Chicago Press, 1916.

"The City of the West Is Dead!"

Bales, Richard. *The Great Chicago Fire and the Myth of Mrs. O'Leary's Cow.* Jefferson, North Carolina: McFarland & Co., 2002.

The great Chicago fire, October 8–10, 1987, Described by Eight Men and Women Who Experienced its Horrors and Testified to the Courage of its Inhabitants. Introduction and Notes by Paul M. Angle. The Chicago Historical Society, 1971.

"How it Originated: Statements and Affidavits to the Starting Point of the Great Fire," *Chicago Tribune,* October 20, 1871.

Loesch, Frank J. *Personal Experiences During the Chicago Fire, 1871.* Chicago: Privately printed, 1925.

Mills, Steve. "Mrs. O'Leary, Cow Cleared by City Council Committee," *Chicago Tribune,* October 6, 1997, p. 2.

Reminiscences of Chicago During the Great Fire, with an Introduction by Mabel McIlvaine. Chicago: R. R. Donnelley & Sons Company, 1915.

Confined against Her Will

Baker, Jean H. *Mary Todd Lincoln: A Biography.* New York: Norton, 1987.

Chicago Daily Tribune articles, March 6, 1867–October 7, 1867, and May 21, 1875–September 12, 1875.

Emerson, Jason, "The Madness of Mary Lincoln," *American Heritage,* June/July 2006. www.americanheritage.com/articles/magazine/ah/2006/3/2006_3_56.shtml (accessed December 2, 2007).

Gernon, Blaine Brooks. *The Lincolns in Chicago.* Chicago: Ancarthe Publishers, 1934.

Helm, Katherine. *The True Story of Mary, Wife of Lincoln: Containing the Recollections of Mary Lincoln's Sister Emilie (Mrs. Ben Hardin Helm), Extracts from Her War-time Diary, Numerous Letters and Other Documents Now First Published by Her Niece, Katherine Helm.* New York: Harper and Brothers, Publishers, 1928. www.questia.com/PM.qst?a=o&d=98844042 (accessed March 14, 2008).

Neely, Mark E., and R. Gerald McMurtry. *The Insanity File: The Case of Mary Todd Lincoln.* Carbondale: Southern Illinois University Press, 1993. www.questia.com/PM.qst?a=o&d=51562224 (accessed December 23, 2007).

Simmons, Dawn Langley. *A Rose for Mrs. Lincoln.* Boston: Beacon Press, 1970.

Atrocious Acts

Avrich, Paul. *The Haymarket Tragedy.* Princeton, New Jersey: Princeton University Press, 1984.

Chicago Tribune articles, May 4–7, 1886, and November 12–13, 1886.

Crain, Caleb. "Haymarket: The Terror Last Time," *The New Yorker*, March 13, 2006.

"The Dramas of Haymarket." Chicago Historical Society Web site. www.chicagohistory.org/dramas/ (accessed September 2, 2008).

Green, James, "Remembering Haymarket: Chicago's Labor Martyrs and Their Legacy," in *Taking History to Heart: The Power of the Past in Building Social Movements.* Amherst: University of Massachusetts Press, 2000.

Hull, Paul C. *The Chicago Riot: A Record of the Terrible Scenes of May 4, 1886. By Paul C. Hull, An Eye-Witness of the Tragedy.* Chicago: Belford, Clarke & Co., 1886. http://libsysdigi.library .uiuc.edu/oca/Books2007-10/chicagoriotrecor00hull/ (accessed September 24, 2008).

Smith, Carl. *Urban Disorder and the Shape of Belief.* The University of Chicago Press, 1995.

A Genuine Refuge

Addams, Jane. *Twenty Years at Hull-House: With Autobiographical Notes.* Illustrated by Norah Hamilton. New York: The Macmillan Company, 1910.

Elshtain, Jean Bethke. *Jane Addams and the Dream of American Democracy: A Life.* New York: Basic Books, 2002.

Jane Addams Hull House Association Web site. www.hullhouse
.org/ (accessed September 20, 2008).

Hovde, Jane. *Jane Addams.* New York: Facts on File, 1989.

Polacheck, Hilda Satt. *I Came a Stranger: The Story of a Hull-House
Girl.* Urbana: University of Illinois Press, 1989.

"The Very Essence of American Progress"

Appelbaum, Stanley. *The Chicago World's Fair of 1893: A
Photographic Record.* New York: Dover Publications, Inc., 1980.

Burnham, Clara Louise. *Sweet Clover: A Romance of the White City.*
Cambridge: The Riverside Press, 1895. http://womenwriters
.library.emory.edu/genrefiction/cti-tgfwfw-cbsweet_016
(accessed October 8, 2008.)

Chicago Daily Tribune articles, June 1892.

Muccigrosso, Robert. *Celebrating the New World: Chicago's
Columbian Exposition of 1893.* Chicago: Ivan R. Dee, 1993.

New York Times articles, July–November 1889, and February–
March 1890.

Rose, Julie K. "The World's Columbian Exposition: Idea,
Experience, Aftermath." Master's thesis, University of Virginia,
August 1, 1996. http://xroads.virginia.edu/~MA96/WCE/title
.html (accessed October 10, 2008).

Rydell, Robert W. "World's Columbian Exposition (May 1,
1893–October 30, 1893)," *The Electronic Encyclopedia of
Chicago.* Chicago Historical Society, 2005. www.encyclopedia
.chicagohistory.org/pages/1386.html (accessed October 10,
2008).

White, Trumbull, and William Ingleheart. *The World's Columbian
Exposition, Chicago, 1893.* Boston: John K. Hastings, 1893.

"Sewed Up His Heart"

Buckler, Helen. *Daniel Hale Williams, Negro Surgeon.* New York: Pitman Publishing Corp., 1968.

Cobb, William. "Dr. Daniel Hale Williams," *Journal of the National Medical Association* 45(5): 379–85, September 1953.

Olivier, Albert F., MD. "Classics in Thoracic Surgery. In Proper Perspective: Daniel Hale Williams, M.D." *The Annals of Thoracic Surgery* 37(1): 96–97, January 1984.

The Provident Foundation Web site. www.providentfoundation .org/ (accessed March 29, 2008).

"Sewed Up His Heart," *Daily Inter Ocean*, July 22, 1893, p. 8.

Shumacker, Jr., Harris B. *The Evolution of Cardiac Surgery.* Indianapolis: Indiana University Press, 1992.

The Race of the Century

"The Automobile," *New York Times* editorial, August 23, 1897, p. 4.

Chicago Times Herald articles, July–November 1895.

"Duryea Motocycle Wins the Race," *Chicago Daily Tribune,* November 29, 1895, p. 8.

Kohlsaat, H. H. "America's First Horseless Carriage Race, 1895," *The Saturday Evening Post*, January 5, 1924, p. 21.

Scharchburg, Richard P. *Carriages without Horses: J. Frank Duryea and the Birth of the American Automobile Industry.* Warrendale, Pennsylvania: Society of Automotive Engineers, 1993.

Scott, Cord. "The Race of the Century—1895 Chicago," *Journal of the Illinois State Historical Society* 96, no. 1, Spring 2003, pp. 37–48.

The Fall of the Sausage King

"A.L. Luetgert is Dead," *Chicago Daily Tribune*, July 28, 1899, p. 7.

Baumann, Edward, and John O'Brien. "The sausage factory mystery," *Chicago Tribune,* August 3, 1986, p. H16.

Chicago Daily Tribune articles, May–October 1897 and December 1897–February 1898.

Loerzel, Robert. *Alchemy of Bones: Chicago's Luetgert Murder Case of 1897.* Urbana: University of Illinois Press, 2003.

The Captain's War

Ballard, E. G. *Captain Streeter, Pioneer.* Chicago: Emery Publishing Service, 1914.

Broomell, Kenneth F., and Harlow M. Church. "Streeterville Saga," *Journal of the Illinois State Historical Society* XXXIII, no. 2, June 1940.

"Captain George Wellington Streeter: Battling Hero of the 'Deestrick of Lake Michigan,'" *Journal of the Illinois State Historical Society* XIII, no. IV, January 1921.

Chicago Daily Tribune articles, May 1899–January 1921.

Salzmann, Joshua. "The Chicago Lakefront's Last Frontier: The Turnerian Mythology of Streeterville, 1886–1961," *Journal of Illinois History* 9, no. 3, Autumn 2006.

Tessendorf, K. C. "Captain Streeter's District of Lake Michigan," *Chicago History, The Magazine of the Chicago Historical Society* V, no. 3, Fall 1976.

His New Job

Bernstein, Arnie. *Hollywood on Lake Michigan: 100 Years of Chicago and the Movies.* Chicago: Lake Claremont Press, 1998.

Chaplin, Charlie. *My Autobiography.* New York: Simon and Schuster, 1964.

Jahant, Charles A. "Chicago: Center of the Silent Film Industry." *Chicago History* III, no. 1, Spring/Summer 1974, pp. 45–53.

Kelly, Kitty. "Flickerings from Film Land," *Chicago Daily Tribune,* February 2, 1915, p. 10.

Loerzel, Robert. "Reel Chicago," *Chicago Magazine,* May 2007. www.chicagomag.com/Chicago-Magazine/May-2007/Reel-Chicago/ (accessed April 12, 2008).

Tinee, Mae, "Charles Chaplin, a Modest Violet, Scared to Death of Publicity." *Chicago Daily Tribune,* January 10, 1915, p. E7.

A Terrible Time

Bonansinga, Jay. *The Sinking of the Eastland: America's Forgotten Tragedy.* New York: Citadel Press (Kensington Publishing Corp.), 2004.

Chicago Tribune articles, July 25, 1915–July 31, 1915 and July 25, 2008.

Dillon, Karen. "Remembering The Eastland—Plaque Honors Victims, Heroes of Maritime Tragedy," *Chicago Tribune,* June 5, 1989, North Sports Final Edition, Chicagoland Section, p. 1.

Eastland Disaster Historical Society Web site. www.eastland disaster.org (accessed December 25, 2007).

Hilton, George W. *Eastland: Legacy of the Titanic.* Palo Alto, CA: Stanford University Press, 1995.

Owens-Schiele, Elizabeth. "Son honors dad by keeping Eastland alive," *Chicago Tribune,* July 25, 2008, North Shore-Metro, p. 3.

Wachholz, Ted, et al. *The Eastland Disaster (Images of America).* Arcadia Publishing, 2005.

"Say It Ain't So!"

Asinof, Eliot. *Eight Men Out: The Black Sox and the 1919 World Series.* New York: Henry Holt and Company, 1963.

Chicago Daily Tribune articles, October 7, 1919–July 10, 1921.

Christgau, John. "Roly and the Alderman: A Small Boy and the Black Sox," *Nine: A Journal of Baseball History and Culture* 13, no. 2, Spring 2005.

Nathan, Daniel A. *Saying It's So: A Cultural History of the Black Sox Scandal.* Urbana and Chicago: University of Illinois Press, 2003.

New York Times articles, September 21, 1919–December 19, 1919.

Seymour, Harold. *Baseball: The Golden Age.* Oxford: Oxford University Press, 1989.

Truth, Justice, and the *Daily News*

Chicago Daily News articles, May 22–31, 1924.

Chicago Daily Tribune articles, May 21, 1924–September 11, 1924.

Darrow, Clarence. *The Story of My Life.* New York: Charles Scribner's Sons, 1932.

Higdon, Hal. *The Crime of the Century: The Leopold and Loeb Case.* Champaign: University of Illinois Press, 1999.

Hohenberg, John. *The Pulitzer Prize Story.* New York: Columbia University Press, 1959.

Leopold, Nathan F., Jr. *Life Plus 99 Years.* Westport, Connecticut: Greenwood Press, 1958.

McPhaul, John J. *Deadlines and Monkeyshines: The Fabled World of Chicago Journalism.* Englewood Cliffs, New Jersey: Prentice-Hall, Inc., 1962.

"We Must Have Tickets!"

Carroll, John M. *Red Grange and the Rise of Modern Football.* Champaign: University of Illinois Press, 1999.

Chicago Daily Tribune articles, November 19–27, 1925.

Daley, Arthur. "Sports of The Times: Forgotten Art," *New York Times,* July 5, 1968, p. 30.

Grange, Red, and Ira Morton. *The Red Grange Story: An Autobiography (As Told to Ira Morton).* Champaign: University of Illinois Press, 1993.

Peterson, Robert W. *Pigskin: The Early Years of Pro Football.* Oxford: Oxford University Press, 1997.

"Red Grange's Claim to Fame," *New York Times,* December 5, 1925, p. 18.

Schwartz, Larry. "Galloping Ghost scared opponents." http://espn .go.com/sportscentury/features/00014213.html (accessed May 11, 2008).

"My Son Was Not a Gangster"

Bergreen, Laurence. *Capone: The Man and the Era.* New York: Simon & Schuster, 1994.

Chicago Daily Tribune articles, February 15, 1929–April 15, 1929.

Helmer, William J., and Arthur J. Bilek. *The St. Valentine's Day Massacre: The Untold Story of the Gangland Bloodbath that Brought Down Al Capone.* Nashville: Cumberland House, 2004.

Kobler, John. *Capone: The Life and World of Al Capone.* Cambridge, Massachusetts: Da Capo Press, 2003.

Journey to a New World

Allardice, Corbin, and Edward R. Trapnell. "The First Pile," *Nuclear News*, November 2002.

Atkins, Stephen E. *Historical Encyclopedia of Atomic Energy.* Westport, Connecticut: Greenwood Press, 2000.

Carey, John. "Enrico Fermi: Unleashing the Atom," *Business Week*, April 5, 2004.

Cronin, James W., ed. *Fermi Remembered.* University of Chicago Press, 2004.

Fermi, Enrico. "The Development of the First Chain Reacting Pile," *Proceedings of the American Philosophical Society* 90, no. 1, January 1946.

———. "Fermi's Own Story," *Chicago Sun-Times*, November 23, 1952.

Fermi, Laura. *Atoms in the Family: My Life with Enrico Fermi.* University of Chicago Press, 1954.

The $5,000 Reward

Bernstein, Arnie. *Hollywood on Lake Michigan: 100 Years of Chicago & the Movies.* Chicago: Lake Claremont Press, 1998.

Chicago Daily Tribune articles, December 1932, November 1933, and August 1945.

McPhaul, John J. *Deadlines and Monkeyshines: The Fabled World of Chicago Journalism.* Englewood Cliffs, New Jersey: Prentice-Hall, Inc., 1962.

"The Reward," *Time*, August 27, 1945. www.time.com/time/magazine/article/0,9171,792330,00.html (accessed March 17, 2008).

Sawyers, June. "The true story that led to Call Northside 777," *Chicago Tribune* Sunday Magazine, Final Edition, C, March 19, 1989.

Warden, Rob, "Joseph M. Majczek," Northwestern University School of Law, Bluhm Legal Clinic, Center on Wrongful Convictions. www.law.northwestern.edu/wrongfulconvictions/ exonerations/ilMajczekSummary.html (accessed March 25, 2008).

No Curses in Baseball?

Bowen, Fred. "For Cubs, a Swing at the Billy Goat Curse." Washington Post, July 17, 2008. www.washingtonpost.com (accessed August 11, 2008).

Castle, George. "This Curse is Foiled! Truth puts Cubs' Billy Goat hex out to pasture." www.yoursportsfan.com/forum (accessed July 29, 2008).

Chicago Daily Tribune articles, September 27, 1945–October 10, 1945.

Chicago Times articles, October 6–10, 1945.

Chicago Tribune. "Oh, Cubs, no," October 6, 2008, p. 28.

Gatto, Steve. *Da Curse of the Billy Goat: The Chicago Cubs, Pennant Races, and Curses.* Lansing, Michigan: Protar House, 2004.

Hooker, Sara. "Can Act of Congress Reverse Curse?" *Daily Herald,* April 23, 2004, p. 1.

Kogan, Rick. *A Chicago Tavern: a Goat, a Curse, and the American Dream.* Chicago: Lake Claremont Press, 2006.

Reaves, Joseph A. "Cubs' Streak Starting to Get Manager's Goat," *Chicago Tribune,* April 30, 1994, p. 3.

A Tale of Two Hoffmans

Chiasson, Lloyd Jr., ed. *The Press on Trial: Crimes and Trials as Media Events.* Westport, Connecticut: Greenwood Press, 1997. www.questia.com/PM.qst?a=o&d=15108466 (accessed November 5, 2007).

Chicago Tribune articles, August 28–30, 1968.

Farber David. *Chicago '68.* University of Chicago Press, 1988.

Kusch, Frank. *Battleground Chicago: The Police and the 1968 Democratic National Convention.* Westport, Connecticut: Praeger, 2004. www.questia.com/PM.qst?a=o&d=106700383 (accessed November 5, 2007).

Lukas, J. Anthony. *The Barnyard Epithet and Other Obscenities: Notes on the Chicago Conspiracy Trial.* New York: Harper & Row, Publishers, Inc., 1970.

New York Times articles, October–December 1969 and February– May 1970.

Rubin Jerry. *We Are Everywhere: Written in the Cook County Jail.* New York: Harper and Row, 1971.

United States of America v. David T. Dellinger et al. No. 18295. United States Court of Appeals for the Seventh Circuit 472 F.2d 340; 1972 U.S. App. LEXIS 6620. February 8, 1972, Argued. November 21, 1972, Decided. www.law.umkc.edu/faculty/projects/ftrials/Chicago7/USvDellinger.htm (accessed September 9, 2008).

Wiener, John, ed. *Conspiracy in the Streets: The Extraordinary Trial of the Chicago Eight.* New York: The New York Press, 2006.

A New Face

Anderson, Jon. "Ch. 7 'hit' parade brings bitterness and better ratings," *Chicago Tribune*, February 14, 1984, Section 5D, p. 1.

———. "Wingin' it with Ch. 7's Oprah Winfrey," *Chicago Tribune*, March 13, 1984, Section 5D, p. 1.

Garson, Helen S. *Oprah Winfrey: A Biography*. Westport, Connecticut: Greenwood Press, 2004.

King, Norman. *Everybody Loves OPRAH!: Her Remarkable Life Story*. New York: William Morrow and Company, Inc., 1988.

Knowles, Francine. "Becoming Oprah: The mogul tells her story, urges women to own themselves," *Chicago Sun-Times*, September 29, 2006, p. 52.

Mair, George. *Oprah Winfrey: The Real Story*. Secaucus, New Jersey: Carol Publishing Group, 1998.

Owen, Mary. "Winfrey fans line up for final Olympic event: season premiere," *Chicago Tribune*, August 31, 2008, p. 3.

Waldron, Robert. *Oprah!* New York: St. Martin's Press, 1991.

Launching a Career

Chicago Tribune articles, January–May 1990.

Culkin, Kit. *I Don't Think So: Confessions of the Stage Father from Hell.* 2006. www.culkinonline.com (accessed December 31, 2007).

Dougherty, Margot. "Big Kid: Macaulay Culkin's Success," *Entertainment Weekly*, no. 43, December 7, 1990. www.ew.com/ew/article/0,,318804,00.html (accessed September 11, 2008).

Internet Movie Database Web site. www.imdb.com/.

Terry, Clifford. "Youngest Stars Always Shine Brightest—Bouncing Off the Walls with Mack," *Chicago Tribune*, November 24, 1991, p. 10 (Arts).

Spitting Images

Chicago Tribune articles, July–August 2004, January–August 2005, April–May 2006, April–June 2007.

"Crown Fountain: One-of-a-Kind Project Combines Art and Tech," *ARCHI-TECH magazine*, July/August 2005. http://www.architechmag.com/articles/detail.aspx?ContentID=2622 (accessed October 11, 2008).

Gilfoyle, Timothy J. *Millennium Park: Creating a Chicago Landmark.* University of Chicago Press, 2006.

Manning, John. E-mail correspondence, October 2008.

Millennium Park Web site. www.millenniumpark.org.

Nance, Kevin. "Have you seen this face?" *The Chicago Sun-Times*, June 24, 2007, p. A13.

Nunn, Emily. "Making Faces—How the Millennium Park fountain designers employed a dentist chair, Sony HDW-F900 and hundreds of curious Chicagoans to pull off this artistic and technological marvel," *Chicago Tribune*, January 27, 2005.

INDEX

ABOUT THE AUTHOR

Scotti McAuliff Cohn is a freelance writer and copyeditor who was born and raised in Springfield, Illinois. She has written five other books for The Globe Pequot Press: *Liberty's Children: Stories of Eleven Revolutionary War Children*, *Beyond Their Years: Stories of Sixteen Civil War Children*, *Disasters and Heroic Rescues of North Carolina*, *It Happened in North Carolina*, and *More than Petticoats: Remarkable North Carolina Women*. She lives in Bloomington, Illinois, with her husband, Ray.